PENGUIN BOOKS

MANOJ AND BABLI

Chander Suta Dogra, earlier with *Outlook* magazine and now with *The Hindu*, has covered North India for two decades. She has travelled extensively in the heartlands of Haryana, Punjab, Himachal Pradesh and Jammu and Kashmir for investigative reporting, often at great risk to herself, on issues ranging from caste and women to the agricultural crisis. This is her first book.

MANOJ AND BABLI
A HATE STORY

CHANDER SUTA DOGRA

PENGUIN BOOKS
An imprint of Penguin Random House

PENGUIN BOOKS

USA | Canada | UK | Ireland | Australia
New Zealand | India | South Africa | China | Singapore

Penguin Books is part of the Penguin Random House group of companies whose addresses can be found at global.penguinrandomhouse.com

Published by Penguin Random House India Pvt. Ltd
4th Floor, Capital Tower 1, MG Road,
Gurugram 122 002, Haryana, India

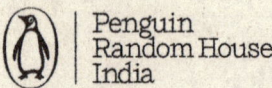

Penguin
Random House
India

First published by Penguin Books India 2013

10 9 8 7 6 5 4 3 2

ISBN 9780143420804

Typeset in Sabon Roman MT by SÜRYA, New Delhi

Printed at Repro India Limited

www.penguin.co.in

FSC
www.fsc.org
MIX
Paper from
responsible sources
FSC® C047271

This is a legitimate digitally printed version of the book and therefore might not have certain extra finishing on the cover.

To Mandvi and Tigmanshu,
my children

Contents

Preface

The first time I encountered an honour killing was in 2004, in a village near Meham, in the heartland of Haryana. A girl had been done to death by her father and brothers for eloping with a boy from a neighbouring village. When I went to her house, I found that the only one who was grieving for the girl and even prepared to say that she had been 'killed' was her mother. The woman, who had probably seen her little girl being throttled to death, was distraught, but lacked the courage to defy her family and walk up to the police station two kilometres away to lodge a complaint.

She found in me a ready punching bag to vent an impotent fury. 'Where were you when my girl was being killed? Where were all these questions that you are directing at me now?' I was confronted with the typical dilemma of a reporter: of how far I should probe to uncover the crime, knowing that it would mean scraping at layers of her still-raw wounds. Her raging helplessness remained with me for a long time, as I subsequently covered many more such incidents over the years.

With North India as my beat in *Outlook*—the weekly newsmagazine where I worked, till recently—I travelled extensively through Haryana, western Uttar Pradesh and Punjab, documenting cases, analysing causes and seeking countless opinions as I tried to comprehend the problem. Then, just when I thought I had explored the modern-day recurrence and spread of honour crimes from every possible angle, I received a call from Kamini Mahadevan of Penguin Books India.

She wanted me to do a book on honour killings and my first impulse was to refuse. What else could I possibly write on the subject? I had already written everything I knew in my articles, and to churn out another 70,000 words seemed quite impossible. Besides, how would I find the time for it? I already had my hands full, covering four states for *Outlook*. I discussed the offer with Ajith Pillai, the then senior editor at the magazine, who urged me to take it. He told me that I could do the research for the book along with my routine reporting and take a few months off to pen the manuscript. The next step was to convince Vinod Mehta, my editor, to give me leave for a few months towards the end. He readily agreed and now I really had no reason to dither.

This was in 2010, the year a sessions court in Karnal had delivered a landmark judgement in the well-known Manoj–Babli honour killing. For the first time, a court had sentenced to death those accused of killing for the sake of honour. I completely missed reporting on this important development because I was doing stories from other states the month the judgement came. By the time I returned to Haryana, newspapers had finished doing editorials on the judgement. Perhaps it was ordained that I would approach this case more comprehensively because the more I looked at this story, the more I realized that it should be my book. That, in hindsight, was the easy part.

*

Haryana is not a reporter's delight. It is hard to ferret out information here and at the best of times villagers can be taciturn, even suspicious of outsiders asking questions.

You could be asking for serious trouble if you happen to pry into their social customs and traditions, especially something touchy like honour crimes. It took me about a year to research this book. From establishing contact with the families of Manoj and Babli, the couple who was killed for marrying into the same gotra, or sub-caste, to getting into the minds of khap leaders in order to understand their motivations.

The more I dug into the story, the more I realized that it was really the heroic struggle of two women, Seema and Chandrapati, who fought against debilitating odds to bring those responsible for the deaths of this young couple to justice. Both the women shared their hopes and struggles, their hardship and fears with me in person and in countless late-night phone conversations (which I continue to have with them). Late night, because that is the only time they can spare for lengthy recollections of their journey.

Seema, Manoj's sister, is a constable with the Haryana police, presently posted in the Madhuban police academy, and has a security cover at all times. She told me over the phone that if I wanted to meet her at the academy, where she has a small government flat, I would need permission from her superiors. I worked the channels from the office of the director general of police (DGP) downwards but the police officers would not let me meet her there. We eventually worked out a system. She would tell me when she was going to her village, Karoran, for the weekend and I would drive down from Chandigarh to meet the family.

I always visited during the afternoon siesta, when few people are about. I took care not to go to Chandrapati's house directly. The caution was rooted in my first experience of the village when I ran into a mixed bunch of young and old men playing cards under a tree. I had sought to draw them into a conversation about the 'honour killing' that had taken place in their village, but was curtly put in my place. 'Behenji, ask us anything else about the village, but not about this case. It's a matter of our village honour and we are not prepared to discuss it with you,' they said. Just like that. A deadpan delivery, tinged with menace. I changed tack and asked for the sarpanch. Accompanied by the sarpanch's mother, I made my way to the house of Babli, hoping to speak to her mother, Ompati. She was plainly hostile: she all but threw me out of her house, warning me never to come there again.

I was also unable to meet the men lodged in Ambala jail, convicted by the courts for the killings, mainly because no official wanted to take the risk of allowing me to meet them. The convicts, who had once been feted across the state for upholding community honour, are today living an ignominious life in jail. It is a sore point with community leaders, and officials are wary of doing anything that can upset the dominant caste. So my requests to officers in the chief minister's office and downwards, till the Ambala district administration, were politely ignored.

I did, however, get lucky with Gangaraj, a Congress worker, widely believed to be the mastermind behind the crime, who was convicted by the Karnal court but subsequently acquitted by the Punjab and Haryana High Court for want of sufficient evidence. He had just returned to Karoran after doing three years in jail, and once again I routed my request to meet him through the sarpanch. I was in luck. Gangaraj, who has refused to meet any journalist after being released from jail, agreed to meet me. But no tape recorders. 'I could have refused and said I am not at home. So don't record this conversation,' he said to me. The man whose activities had held all of Haryana in thrall for almost two years told me that he has given up politics because the party had not stood by him. He was bitter and withdrawn. While researching Gangaraj, I chanced upon two videos taken by the local stringer of CNN-IBN, a national channel, which featured the man.

But my task was to reconstruct not just the killing of Manoj and Babli but also its impact in the Haryana countryside. For the first, I have relied on the prosecution's case in the Karnal sessions court. I procured court petitions, copies of first information reports (FIRs), testimonies of witnesses and more.

As for the second, which was to capture the pressures and persuasions taking place outside the courts, I gathered video recordings of events from local stringers and amateur documentary makers. Many of these video recordings had been broadcast on television channels when this crime was being intensively reported in the media. I discovered that intrepid local journalists had recorded important khap meetings in the villages, in which significant decisions about this and other cases were taken. These videos were invaluable in reconstructing meetings of khap panchayats, what was said there and the atmosphere that prevailed in these meetings, all of which helped me get a sense of the depth of passions at play in those months. Then there were hundreds of newspaper clippings, which covered every little development of the saga playing out in the countryside. These too I sourced from activists of the Janwadi Mahila Samiti (JMS), the Democratic Youth Federation of India (DYFI), and some from Seema and Narinder.

I also met and interviewed scores of other people connected with the case, many of who figure in the book. They gave freely of their time and I am deeply indebted to them. While the names of the main characters are all real, some of the other names have been changed. Almost all the events in the book are true, except the atmospherics employed in reconstructing the story.

*

This book would never have been completed without the help and insights given by Jagmati Sangwan, the walking encyclopedia on honour crimes in North India, and her husband, Inderjeet; my editor Kamini Mahadevan, who held my hand throughout its gestation with her unobtrusive suggestions and knack of keeping me focused through bouts of uncertainty; my dear friend Meera Ranjan, who read the manuscript as often as I asked her to—I owe much of the shape of this book to her valuable advice; Ajith Pillai for showing me the way; and Vinod Mehta's encouraging presence; my daughter, Mandvi, whose forthright comments have helped to smoothen the narrative; Roddy Mackenzie, H. Kishie Singh, Smita Kumar and many people in Haryana whom I cannot name. They know who they are and what their contribution to making this book as authentic as possible is.

Prologue

Om Prakash was worried about his paddy crop. The water level in the Balsamand Minor canal had dipped over the past two days and if it did not rise soon he would have to use his brother's tube well for a day. It was June. With the power supply limited to four hours a day, he would have to spend at least a thousand rupees to buy diesel for the genset he shared with his brothers. Between them, they owned a respectable tract of land in their village, Sandlana.

It was late afternoon when he downed a cup of tea and set off for the canal. Even before he reached there, he sensed the canal had no water, because the familiar chill there was missing. As the silted bed of the canal came into view, Om Prakash realized that the release of water into Balsamand Minor had been stopped altogether.

The Bhakra mainline canal system has been bringing the Sutlej waters to parched parts of western Haryana since the Bhakra Dam was constructed in the 1960s. The state was then a part of joint Punjab, which was reorganized in 1966 to form the present three states of Haryana, Punjab and Himachal Pradesh. Sections of the canal network date back to British times.

One of the many irrigation channels branching like a web from the Bhakra Dam, the Balsamand Minor snakes eastwards from the Barwala main branch and runs through a score of villages in Narnaund subdivision of Hisar district.

When water is low in the Barwala canal, the Sirsa branch canal, carrying waters from the Western Yamuna Canal system, replenishes it. This did not happen on that day.

The south-west monsoon had not yet hit Haryana but the humidity in the air was stifling. The smell of decaying wood and vegetation hung heavily in the air. Stumps of fallen branches, swept in by the flow, lay in knots on the slushy canal bed. Om Prakash turned his head to look upstream. The unmistakable smell of rotting flesh filled his nostrils. His eyes searched for the carcass of a dog or a buffalo. They alighted instead on a pair of human legs bound together with a rope. He stepped closer and saw a bloated body of what looked like a woman, stuck in a pile of leaves and slush. Scraps of clothing still clung to it; though he wanted to go nearer for a look, the stench made him gag. The body had surfaced only because the water in the canal had receded, he thought, as he hurried back towards Sandlana to alert the village chowkidar, Karambir.

Karambir, one of the few belonging to the Valmiki caste in their predominantly upper-caste Jat village, was proud of his job and the responsibility it entailed. As soon as he heard of this body in the Balsamand canal, he set off for Kapdo to inform the police. By the time darkness fell, the rotting body of a woman had been pulled out of the canal. A crowd of curious villagers gathered around it while a handful of policemen from Kapdo took charge. The police photographer was taking pictures from all angles. The disfigured face, the bald, peeling scalp, with bits of hair stuck to it, the maggots crawling on the flesh and lastly the rope around her feet. People who looked closely noticed that she had been wearing a green kurta and a black salwar. Only the police knew that this was the second body that was pulled out from Balsamand Minor that day.

Earlier in the day, someone had reported the sighting of a

dead body at Kheri Chopta, a few kilometres downstream. The Kheri chowkidar, Krishana, had ascertained that it was the body of a young man, before cycling to the Kheri police station to inform them. Within the hour the police arrived in a dung-coloured jeep. The man's body was wrapped in a whitish sack. The people who helped pull it out of the canal concluded the body had been wrapped in it before being thrown into the water. The torn clothes had blood on them and a knotted rope was looped twice round the neck, with the ends being used to bind his feet together. The sub-inspector (SI) heading the police party said a few words to Krishana, who was now part of the crowd—all men and boys—which had gathered like vultures around the body. Krishana went towards the village and returned with a tractor that had a trolley trailing behind. They put the sack containing the body on the trolley; as the police jeep and tractor passed through the outer circle of Kheri Chopta on the road to Narnaund, the womenfolk caught a glimpse of it. That night, the only talk around the hookahs in at least ten villages near the Balsamand canal was about the discovery of the bodies. Two people had been brutally killed and thrown into the canal. When? No one knew. Who were they? Were they a couple? Doomed lovers? Were the two deaths linked?

Part One

Love and Death

Chapter One

'The Police Is Protecting Us'

11.30 a.m., 15 June 2007

The sight of litigants crowding the court and the overall bustle made her feel better. It gave her an odd sense of security. A posse of policemen stood there to protect them of course, but it was only when the magistrate began recording her statement that the queasiness in her stomach began to ebb. Perhaps it was the munsif's detached manner, the magistrate's indifferent gaze or the official air of the courtroom where her statement was being recorded as a routine procedure that led Babli to believe the worst was over. Her face glowed as she stated for the record that she had married Manoj of her own will. Her voice was low but clear. The beautiful eyes, which had charmed the young and not so young in her village, flashed now and then. It took all of ten minutes and soon they were out in the dappled sunshine streaming through the laburnum trees, which seemed to embrace the drab court building in a golden clasp. Her heart sang.

Manoj squeezed her arm and she sighed in relief. They exchanged a quick glance and the police constable nearest to her motioned them towards a waiting Gypsy. But Babli wanted a cup of tea badly. The two of them hadn't had a morsel since morning and, now that their statements had been recorded without incident, she suddenly felt hungry. As she turned to tell Manoj that they should stop at one of the grimy tea stalls that dotted the court complex, she saw them. The realization that they were here hit her hard. She immediately recognized Gurdev in his familiar white kurta pyjama and two other cousins confabulating with him. Suresh, her darling brother, with his mop of unruly hair, which till a few days back she had loved to ruffle, stood a little way off. Quite unexpectedly he looked up from the cell phone in his hand and their eyes met. Babli shivered at the hatred she saw in them. His usual playful expression had disappeared. He also seemed older than his twenty-two years, with his taut and drawn face and the darkening stubble on his chin. For a moment she wondered if it was indeed him. But when her chacha, Rajinder, joined him and they all began following her with their eyes, she instinctively moved closer to Manoj for support. She could sense her husband's uneasiness as they walked quietly towards the Gypsy, accompanied by the policemen from Rajaund, the police station under which their village, Karoran, fell. Her new anklets tinkled and she had a sudden urge to hide the red glass bangles she was wearing on her wrists and forearms.

As they passed the group, Gurdev stepped forward to speak to her. 'What is done is done, Babli. I want to tell you that if you have any problem, you must let us know.' She moved as if in slow motion. After the days of uncertainty, hiding from the family and marrying Manoj in a Chandigarh temple, Gurdev's friendly words seemed unreal. Bewildered, she looked up, but there was nothing else in his or the others' demeanour to suggest truce. The police party of five constables and a sub-inspector who had been ordered by the court to provide the newly-weds protection was by now getting edgy and they pushed their way through the crowds to get Manoj and Babli into the Gypsy.

Ever since their advocate had told them that they would have to appear before a Kaithal magistrate to make a statement about their marriage, the two had been uneasy. 'It will take just a day,' he assured them. They knew only too well the dangers of leaving the relative security of their small one-room home in Chandigarh and presenting themselves in Kaithal as man and wife. But giving the statement was vital. It would lessen to some extent the harassment and pressure Manoj's widowed mother, Chandrapati, and his two sisters and younger brother, Vinod, were facing for what Manoj had done. A panchayat had been called in the village chaupal, where many of their neighbours and acquaintances suggested that Chandrapati and Vinod be beaten up so that they would reveal the whereabouts of Manoj and Babli. Her uncles had used their influence to get the Rajaund police to register an FIR against Manoj and his mother for kidnapping Babli. It was in connection with that case that Manoj and Babli had been summoned to the court today. Just thinking of what his mother had told him on the phone the night before made him sick. 'If I don't tell them where you two are, they will . . . Hardly anyone talks to us in the village. We are very frightened, beta,' she had sobbed on the phone.

1.20 p.m.

They got down from the police Gypsy at Pehowa bus stand and headed towards a Chandigarh-bound bus. By now the sun was beating down mercilessly. The smell of putrefying garbage from the overflowing bins near the bus stand's boundary assailed Babli's nostrils. Pehowa is a pilgrimage town, thirty-five kilometres north of Kaithal. An array of buses stood in the parking plaza, haphazardly parked. Children yelled excitedly, their mothers struggled with huge bags, and the men sauntered about, their hands in their pockets. 'The heat does not seem to affect the bustling crowd here,' she thought, 'so why should it bother me?' She moved purposefully, gathering the small bag which held a change of clothes and the papers the lawyer had given them. Suddenly she froze.

'They have followed us here,' she whispered urgently. Manoj had also seen them sitting in a red Maruti car. 'Relax, these policemen are guarding us. There's nothing to worry about,' he whispered back, but, inside, fear had begun gnawing at him. The sight of Babli's mama, chacha and cousins, all together, was not propitious. They had booked him for kidnapping Babli. But this morning she had testified before the magistrate that she had gone with Manoj of her own free will and that they were married in accordance with the law. So they were now in the clear. They had taken the precaution of petitioning the court, on their lawyer's advice, to provide them protection from these relatives, which was granted. The illaqua (district) magistrate had recorded Babli's statement under Section 164 of the Code of Criminal Procedure, 1973 (CrPc) and the sessions judge at Kaithal had directed the station house officer (SHO) of Rajaund to provide them security.

But instead of reassuring him, it made Manoj even more uneasy. How for instance did Gurdev, Baru Ram and others know that Babli would be deposing today? Could someone from the police station have informed them? Hadn't his mother and his sister Seema heard that the policemen of Rajaund were hostile and cautioned him on the phone? The nameplate of the policeman nearest to him read Head Constable Jai Inder Singh. Head Constable Dharampal, in civvies, was busy picking his nose as he followed SI Jagbir Singh, who was leading the way to the bus. Constable Usha Rani, Constable Satbir Singh and Head Constable Ram Mehar were walking beside Babli. Jagbir Singh too had noticed the red Maruti following them from Agrasain Chowk in Kaithal. It was parked near the boundary wall, where men usually stopped to urinate, while entering or leaving the bus stand. He asked Ram Mehar to go and check their papers.

'Show me your papers,' said Ram Mehar to the one at the wheel. 'Why were you following our Gypsy? I'm confiscating your papers. You will get them only after we have checked your background.'

The boy at the wheel, who looked to Babli like her cousin Dharamvir from a distance, began to say something when Gangaraj, a Congress activist, appeared on the scene. 'I am Gangaraj,' he growled. 'You cannot take his papers like this.' There seemed to be an argument. Then Gangaraj called up someone. Ram Mehar was contemplating taking the car to the police thana, when Jai Inder Singh sauntered over. 'Let them go, they have talked to SHO sahib,' he told Ram Mehar, all the while scratching his balls. The policemen backed off. Jagbir Singh also called up someone on the phone and after a brief conversation came towards Manoj.

'I am deputing two constables to escort you. They will travel with you and leave you at your destination.'

It was terribly hot inside the bus and they had difficulty finding seats. Almost everyone seemed to be heading towards Chandigarh today. Or were they short-distance commuters? Babli couldn't tell. All she wanted was to flop on a seat and rest her head on Manoj's shoulder. She felt exhausted by the heat and events of the morning and just wanted to get away. Sweat trickled down her back and she could feel her kurta sticking uncomfortably to her skin. The bus announced its departure with a loud horn, scattering the crowd of travellers standing around it. Out of the corner of her eye, Babli could see the red Maruti, HR08G-3689, beginning to move. Manoj and she had found a two-seater at the front end of the bus, and the two policemen, Dharampal and Satbir, took up nearby seats. A sweaty trader and his family had squeezed into the space Manoj and Babli had been standing in, in the aisle. They spoke in whispers. 'Once we reach Chandigarh, things will be fine,' Manoj assured her with a confidence he barely felt himself.

'Have you talked to Amma and informed her that my statement has been recorded?'

'No, I don't have much balance in my phone. I'll call from an STD booth somewhere.'

'It has been more than two months and this nightmare doesn't seem to end. What did the khap panchayat decree? Did Amma say anything about it yesterday?'

'Not Amma. Seema told me that Gangaraj is calling the khap panchayat every other day. Someone from your gali came to our house on Tuesday and threatened Amma and Seema. I wish I was there to help them. There is no man in our house to tell these people off. Vinod is too young. If Dada were alive . . .'

'You think Dada would have agreed to our marriage?' she said incredulously.

'No, silly. He was as much a Banwala Jat as, say, Gangaraj. Who knows what he would have done?'

Some thirty minutes later the bus took a turn and almost at once they hit the busy marketplace of Malikpur. It stopped near a shop crammed with sweets and savouries. Someone was frying samosas near its entrance and Babli again felt hungry. Many people got down and, as she glanced around to see if she had time to quickly buy a couple of samosas, she saw them once again. Two of her cousins were sitting three seats behind them! Manoj too saw them then and the couple was panic-stricken. Her relatives seemed to have come crawling out of the woodwork. The police had to be informed. 'Bhai sahib, Babli's relatives are in the same bus as us. There they are,' he said, nervously turning his head in their direction.

'*Main dekhta hoon,*' said Head Constable Dharampal before speaking to someone on his phone. 'We will have to get down here,' he told Manoj. 'SHO sahib is coming with a Gypsy and we will take you to Pipli in it.'

Between the two of them, Babli and Manoj decided that instead of going to Chandigarh they would head off to Delhi, taking a bus from Pipli. Dharampal concurred. Within minutes of their getting down from the bus, SI Jagbir Singh's Gypsy arrived and once again they got into it. As the Gypsy moved towards Pipli, Manoj noticed Jai Inder Singh whispering into his phone. When he saw Manoj looking at him, he quickly cut the connection and looked out of the window. A few minutes later he was again at it. It made Manoj very anxious. 'Wonder who he is talking to. Could it be Gangaraj?' the thought flashed through his mind. He was glad Babli had not noticed Jai Inder's antics.

The Gypsy swerved to avoid two cows standing aimlessly on the busy road as it swung into Pipli's modest bus stand on Grand Trunk (GT) Road. Just as it came to a halt with its brakes screeching, SI Jagbir rummaged in his pocket and soon produced two sheets of paper, which he thrust towards Manoj.

'The jurisdiction of Kaithal district police ends here, so we will have to leave you. But don't worry, we are keeping an eye on your relatives and have told them not to follow you. They will go back now.'

'But you were to leave us till our destination. We need you to accompany us till Delhi,' Manoj pleaded.

'I have my orders. Please sign these papers which state

that we accompanied you till Pipli.' There was nothing more to be said.

1.30 p.m.

Mandeep had parked his Scorpio all morning outside the civil hospital in Kaithal. It was 1.30 p.m. and hot as hell; he hadn't had a single customer. The civil hospital taxi stand was generally considered to be good for making a quick buck, as the hospital catered to scores of villages around Kaithal. There was always a stream of patients and their attendants who had to be ferried to their villages. Mandeep's boss, the owner of the Scorpio, had paid a hefty sum to the taxi union to get a place here. Mandeep snicked a bidi from his mate, the owner of the tea stall nearby, and had just settled down to enjoy a puff, when six men approached him. The one in a white shirt and pyjama spoke first: '*Ambala ka kya lega?*' What will you take for Ambala?

'*Shyam nu vapas aane hai kya?*' said Mandeep, as he took the last drags from the bidi. He wanted to know if they would return in the evening.

The stout one in a pyjama and shirt stepped in. He seemed to be the leader of the group. Mandeep learned later that he was Gangaraj. 'Listen, we are from Karoran village and our daughter has eloped with a boy from the village. It has brought disrepute to the family and we need a car to go to Ambala and Patiala so that they can be caught and brought back,' he said in a deep voice which commanded immediate attention.

'*Tera sau lagenge, aur tel aapka,*' said Mandeep. You'll have to pay me 1300 rupees and buy the petrol too.

He regarded them with some curiosity. They were not his usual kind of customers. The men exuded urgency. Mandeep could sense it.

'*Chal bhai. Le chal,*' said the wiry one, and they all got into the vehicle. Gangaraj sat next to Mandeep in the front seat.

It was a state highway, fairly well maintained, and they moved at a steady speed. Gangaraj was constantly on the phone. A little ahead of Pehowa, he asked Mandeep to stop the vehicle for a while, to take a phone call. With the engine muted, Mandeep could clearly hear someone telling Gangaraj not to proceed to Ambala, but to go instead to Pipli. They waited there for fifteen minutes and then asked Mandeep to take the road to Pipli. On reaching Pipli bus stand, Mandeep circled it once, then parked the Scorpio on the road outside.

It struck Mandeep as odd that throughout the journey from Kaithal to Pipli, no one had spoken except Gangaraj. He put it down to the tense situation they were in. Being a Jat himself, he could understand their plight. He was beginning to like this assignment. It was much more exciting than ferrying patients. In that short time, he had inexplicably become a participant in the family's chase of their daughter. After the lethargy of the morning, he could feel a surge of adrenalin in his system and was impatient to move on.

All six had got out of the car at Pipli, and he could see Gangaraj talking to someone on a Splendor motorcycle. Three of his passengers then began walking towards Lal Batti Chowk, and ten minutes later Gangaraj received another call in which the caller told him that they were in the bus.

'*Theek ho gaya. Ab jahan bhi bus rukegi, unhon ko bahar nikal liyo. Hum peeche peeche aa rahe hain.*' Everything's going okay. Wherever it stops, get them off the bus. We're following you. Gangaraj spoke into the phone.

He ordered Mandeep to turn the vehicle towards Karnal.

With Gangaraj in the front with him and the remaining two persons in the back seat, they sped away.

3.30 p.m.

Pipli is situated on National Highway No. 1, also called the GT Road. The route is believed to go back to Mauryan times. The present road is more or less the one built by Sher Shah Suri, the sixteenth-century ruler, from Multan in modern-day Pakistan to Sasaram in Bihar. It was called Sadak-e-Azam in those days and milestones, or kos minars (one kos equals three miles approximately), dating from that period can still be seen at several places along this highway. Pipli however draws its prominence from the historic city of Kurukshetra, the battlefield of the epic Mahabharata. The town is a gateway of sorts for Kurukshetra. Situated 160 kilometres north of Delhi, en route to Chandigarh, Pipli is a junction for buses criss-crossing Haryana and others going to and from Chandigarh and Punjab. It has one of the most crowded bus terminuses on the highway. The popular eatery Parakeet, run by the Haryana Tourism Development Corporation, right across it is crowded with travellers at any time of the day.

But today there seemed to be a lull. Perhaps a consequence of the afternoon heat. Abandoned by their police escorts, Manoj and Babli, seeing just a thin crowd at the station, felt terribly exposed and insecure. 'What should we do now?' said Babli, as soon as SI Jagbir moved away.

'We'll have to find a bus for Delhi and hope for the best,' said Manoj as he wiped the sweat from his brow.

'Gurdev and Satish haven't let us out of their sights for a moment. I wonder if the others won't follow us here too,' she fretted.

Manoj looked around for an STD booth and, spotting

one near Parakeet, began walking towards it. 'I have to call up Amma and tell her what has happened. Let's also grab a cup of tea.'

But Babli was out of her mind with worry. She knew her brothers and chacha well. Momentarily, she remembered her mother and longed for her comforting hand. 'Ma will never allow harm to befall me. She loves me a lot,' she thought.

Manoj spoke to his mother for almost ten minutes and told her everything that had transpired since morning; he said they were boarding a bus for Delhi. He asked her to call whenever possible, as he had no balance left in his phone. He felt much better. Now for that tea.

The bus for Delhi was about to leave and they quickly boarded it. It was only half-full and they had no problem finding a seat. Babli cast a quick glance around and was relieved to see that no one had followed them into this bus. She hoped that SI Jagbir Singh had kept his word and warned her relatives not to follow them. They were in a Haryana Roadways bus that belched and burped when it began to pick up speed as it exited the bus stand. Making its way through a tangle of two-wheelers, pedestrians and a tractor trolley turning into a side lane, it headed towards Lal Batti Chowk. It slowed near the chowk from where the road turns on to the Delhi highway, and some more passengers got on. This time Satish, Gurdev and Suresh climbed aboard from the front door. There was a marked change in their demeanour since morning. Bold and confident, they boarded the bus and occupied the two empty seats closest to the couple. The menace emanating from them was palpable. Manoj looked at Babli with concern, but she had covered her head with her green printed dupatta and was looking down at her hands. There wasn't much they could do. Petrified, she was finding it difficult to breathe. She wanted to hold his hand, but dared not.

Manoj opened the window, which immediately let in the hot wind or loo. She tightened the dupatta over her head, and the wind dried the sweat from their bodies. They hadn't exchanged a word. In twenty-odd minutes they were approaching Karnal. From the window they could see an approaching toll plaza under construction. At a signboard on the side of the road that said Arjaheri, the bus slowed down. For a moment Babli toyed with the idea of asking Manoj if they should get down and try to shake them off. On second thoughts, she told herself, 'No, it is safer for us to be in the bus. They can't harm us here with so many people watching.' Her mind raced, seeking ways to escape from her brothers.

Just then a silver-coloured Scorpio swung out from the right and stopped in front of the bus, blocking its way. The driver slammed the brakes to avoid hitting the SUV. Brakes screeched, tyres burnt the tarmac and many passengers popped their heads out of the windows to see what was happening. Babli felt rough hands grabbing her—it was Suresh—and pushing her towards the door. Satish and Gurdev had grabbed Manoj and were dragging him out too. *'Bachao, bachao! Marenge,'* he shouted, but neither the bus driver nor the passengers came to their rescue. It was as if they had been hypnotized. The slightly built Manoj was completely overpowered and, by the time his feet touched the road, they had stuffed something into his mouth to prevent him from shouting.

Babli yelled and screamed until Suresh hit her hard and clamped his hand over her mouth. An earring twisted in the violent struggle and pierced the skin of her jawbone. It took just two minutes for the trio to push Babli and Manoj into the Scorpio, where Gangaraj, Rajinder and others were waiting for them grimly.

Kuldeep, a young graduate who a few months ago had got a contract for earthwork at the toll plaza, had seen the Scorpio forcibly stopping the Haryana Roadways bus. He saw a boy and a screaming, struggling girl being dragged out of the bus and three men pushing them into the Scorpio. He, along with a few other workers present at the spot, rushed to help them. But by then Mandeep had hit the accelerator and the Scorpio raced off. *'Number note karo,'* Kuldeep shouted to someone near him. The number, HR05-M-4748, was scribbled on a palm. He himself had reached close enough to get a good view of both Babli and Manoj. He quickly dialled 100, the police helpline. Then picking up Manoj's right shoe, which had fallen off during the scuffle, he placed it on the ledge of the half-constructed booth on the first lane and decided to wait for the police.

4.30 p.m.

They lay sore and frightened on the floor of the Scorpio. Suresh and Satish crushed them underfoot. Rajinder turned back from the front seat, and spat out the green groggly he had worked up on Babli. *'Haraamzadi,'* he hissed. Suresh's boots were grinding against her red glass bangles, shattering them one by one. Shards from the broken bangles pierced her soft arms and they began to bleed, staining the mat below. She began to sob softly.

Manoj lay curled up on the floor in the boot. His shirt was torn in places and the metal base of the back seat was digging into his clavicle. His oppressors had their feet firmly planted on his back and he had to twist his neck and face in order to breathe. Choking with fear, he retched, but only a thin string of saliva trickled out.

The vehicle took several turns and after about an hour and a half Gangaraj ordered Mandeep to stop. Suresh,

Rajinder, Satish and Gurdev jumped out, dragging Manoj and Babli with them into the fields. The Scorpio drove away with Gangaraj in it. Baru Ram, who was following in his white Maruti HR09-6500, came near them but soon headed towards Karoran. It was around 6 p.m. and the abductors waited for darkness to fall. The newly-weds lay trussed and gagged in a wheat field. Manoj realized with a shock that they had reached the outskirts of Karoran. In the distance was Rahra, the next village on the road, and Bakal a little further off. They were a few yards away from Suresh's fields, which were marked by two twisted kikar trees growing near a drainage ditch.

After about half an hour, Baru Ram and some more people from Karoran joined them. They had with them several coils of stout rope, a gunny bag and sticks. As if their arrival was a signal to get to work, Suresh and Gurdev picked up Manoj and flung him on the ground. He fell with a thud, screaming in pain. They set upon him with fury: *'Saale, behenchod, mhaari izzat duboega ke?'* Bloody sister fucker, so you were going to destroy our honour?

For the next ten minutes the only sound that could be heard was Manoj's cries of pain as several hands and feet bludgeoned him with lathis and kicked him in the face and groin. Rajinder uncoiled the rope and slipped it round Manoj's neck. As Baru Ram, Gurdev and Suresh held him, Rajinder pulled the noose tight. The lifeless heap at their feet did not even feel it tightening around his neck: he had lost consciousness when Baru Ram had cracked a lathi on his temple.

Babli, paralysed with fear, watched them with glazed eyes. The screams welling up inside stuck in her throat. The sight of Manoj's lifeless body and the inevitability of what they would do to her had turned her legs to lead. Whimpering with fear, she slumped on to Suresh, just as her salwar became wet. Gurdev and Baru Ram turned towards her and pinned her down on the ground by the arms. Suresh dug a knee into her chest and poured a bottle of a foul-smelling liquid down her throat. The fumes of Endosulfan, a pesticide commonly used by farmers in the area, spread in the night air and, even before it hit her stomach, the chemical began searing her oesophagus. She gasped and immediately choked on the liquid. The excruciating pain tearing through her insides left her writhing on the earth. *'Bacha le re, bacha le. Maaa! Maaa!'* she screamed into the darkness. A dog barked in the distance.

Saliva foamed around her mouth and her lips, now blue, curled up grotesquely. They watched silently until the writhing became feeble and the cries stopped. Gurdev then tied her hands and feet with a rope. She was dumped into the boot of a car, but they had still not finished with Manoj. Suresh bound his feet and hands in a similar manner and attached a rope from the motionless body to the hook at the back of the car.

The men did not know it then, and later it was said that even if they had it wouldn't have changed anything, but many approving eyes had watched the killings from a discreet distance. They followed the car, with Manoj's body being dragged and Babli's stuffed into the boot, till it faded into the darkness.

Chapter Two

The Girl with the Silver Hoops

So much had happened in the two-odd months since he and Babli had stolen away one breezy April night from their village, Karoran. In all his twenty-three years, he couldn't remember having done anything more exciting. Nothing in life had prepared him for it either.

His father, Satbir Singh, had quit the army after serving as a sepoy for a few years, to return home to join the Haryana police. During Bhajan Lal's term as chief minister, he was laid off because the court had detected an irregularity in the recruitment of his batch. Satbir then took up a job with the water supply department.

When Manoj was only six years old, his father died of a heart attack and since then his grandfather Hari Singh had run the household and paid for the children's education. Hari Singh had served as a subedar in the British army. People in Karoran respected him, even though the family did not own much land. When he came home on retirement, Hari Singh was unanimously elected the village sarpanch for two consecutive terms. He was instrumental in setting up the community centre in Karoran, which doubles as a resting place for wedding parties halting for the night, and bringing the telephone line to the village. He was also responsible for getting the Haryana Roadways bus service to the village. Even today, people in Karoran often remark, *'Bhai, subedar hi kar gaya is gaon mein kaam.'* It is the subedar alone who got something done for this village.

Manoj's mother chipped in by rearing buffaloes, and ever since he could remember, even before his father died, she was the pivot of their family. Like most others of their village, they were Banwala Jats, a landowning martial community who lived by strict social and moral codes. Chandrapati doted on her eldest son, as most Jat mothers do. Manoj had his father's looks, a thick mop of hair flopping over his high cheekbones and a prominent nose. His slim, angular face matched his slight build. His was not a dominating presence, even though as the eldest son he was, in a sense, the 'man' of the house. Unlike his precocious younger brother, Vinod, Manoj was cheerful but reserved. Never boisterous. One rarely heard him raising his voice in the house.

For Chandrapati, he could do no wrong. She barely raised an eyebrow when he failed to clear one paper in the Plus Two exams. For him, studying at Karoran Government Senior Secondary School, just getting through those examinations was tedious. After that one setback, he almost gave up studying. But as the eldest son, it was expected that he should contribute to the household kitty. His father's small pension and the produce from their share of two and a half acres of land were barely enough to meet the family's expenses. So Manoj joined a computer diploma course at Kaithal, the district headquarters, some twenty-five kilometres away, and also took up apprenticeship with Balkar, who ran an electronics repair shop in their village.

Balkar's shop was right across the girls' school and he also ran a busy PCO from it. It was a hub of sorts for youngsters wanting to make calls and Manoj enjoyed the evenings he spent there, learning the ropes of the business.

He wanted to set up a shop of his own and was working hard to achieve his goal. By the time Manoj joined as an apprentice, Babli had passed out of the school.

The first time Babli entered the shop, she was with another girl and they looked around diffidently. Sitting at one end, he was absorbed in repairing a transistor. He knew they would want to make a call and he felt somewhat irritated because the owner of the transistor was due to come for it any moment. Babli's friend made a quick call and paid up the amount given on the slip he handed her. For a while, they lingered outside the shop. Manoj was struck by the way she carried herself. Lithe and tall, with a swinging plait, she had a face that glowed in the evening light. That evening he couldn't concentrate on his dinner. Visions of Babli kept distracting him from the funny story his bright, young sister Seema was relating. It was something about Madho, their sharp-tongued neighbour's buffalo, refusing to allow her to milk it. Their siblings, Rekha and Vinod, were in splits. Chandrapati smiled at them from her usual place by the chulha from where she turned out hot chapattis for all of them.

The next day Babli was back at the shop and wanted him to repair the display on her cell phone. Manoj fiddled with it, but found nothing amiss. Months later she laughingly told him, 'Of course there was nothing wrong with it. I just wanted to see you again.' By then, they were hopelessly in love. Sometimes they met at dusk, in the shadow of the dera or shrine of Nath sadhus, which had stood for centuries on the outskirts of the village. Its high walls, ancient peepul trees and the sadhus there, who went about their tasks unconcerned by their presence, gave them an unfamiliar sense of security. He thought she was the most beautiful creature he had ever set his eyes on: doe-eyed, fair and tall, and with a constant smile on her lips. Mesmerized, he was content to gaze upon her moonlike face while she chattered like a brook. She seemed to draw him to herself. If it was not for her exuberant nature, always looking for new ways to amuse herself and satisfy her curiosity about this or that, he would probably still be repairing broken transistors at his shop. Shy, he couldn't ever approach a girl, unlike many other boys in his school. Babli, on the other hand, was outgoing. She was on the school kabaddi team and had told him how much she enjoyed going to other schools for tournaments. She wanted to graduate from a college in Kaithal and qualify for a government teacher's job. Her father too had died many years ago, and her mother, Ompati, was dependent on the men in the family. A few days after she gave her Class X exams, the elders in her family decreed that her studies were over. She could not go to Kaithal or elsewhere for further studies. Period.

But that did not seem to dampen her enthusiasm for life. Babli loved watching television serials and her addiction to them often surprised him. Once she brought the pirated DVD of an episode that she had missed and wanted him to play it on a customer's player he was repairing. She wouldn't take no for an answer and walked out in a huff when he begged her not to insist. He often wondered how lucky he was to have her love. But meeting her was not always possible, so most times they spoke to each other on the phone. Even that was fraught with risk. Often he caught Seema looking at him curiously when he was talking with Babli. Of all his siblings, he liked Seema the most and was sometimes tempted to confide in her. But each time he tried to do so, he balked because he knew it would horrify the family.

As Seema later told me, Babli was a Banwala Jat like Manoj and, coming as they did from the same village, she was, in the eyes of their community, a sister to him. It was an incestuous match, so unthinkable that when initial murmurings about their growing acquaintance did the rounds in Karoran their mother was dismissive. 'My Manoj is a very sensible boy who knows what is right and wrong. The girl is from our own gotra and he knows there is no future for them,' she had once told Seema in Manoj's hearing.

At around the same time, Manoj's dream of setting up his own repair shop was beginning to take shape. It was just a question of getting his mother to agree.

'Amma, I have talked to the sarpanch about taking one of the shops built by the panchayat on rent,' he informed his mother one evening as she gave the buffaloes the last feed of the day. 'Are you sure this is what you want to do? And, more importantly, have you learned enough from Balkar to set up your own shop?' Chandrapati wanted to know.

'I have been preparing for this for more than a year now, Amma. Let me at least give it a shot. Balkar told me that I have a good hand for repairing electronics. And I have saved some money to equip the shop too. It will be better for me to take a place on the outskirts of the village for greater visibility, but this one is cheaper.'

'If you are adamant on setting up this shop, I insist that you take the one from the panchayat. The area outside is a haven for drunks at night. I don't want them making an adda in your shop,' she said categorically.

Seema, who was home for the weekend from Jaipur where she was pursuing a degree in law, overheard the exchange and made a face. 'Manoj, why don't you study a little more and get a worthwhile job? Once a repair mechanic, always one!' she shouted from inside.

'You do the studying. I have bigger responsibilities. Besides, we need the money,' he retorted.

Chandrapati put away the leftover fodder in a corner of the courtyard, washed her hands and came inside. Seema knew she did not like her opposing Manoj or bringing up his lack of interest in studies. 'He is right. You leave him alone and go and get me a teaspoon of whey from Paro chachi, to set the curds. Rekha forgot to set aside some,' she intervened. It effectively ended the discussion and Manoj's shop sprang to life in the following weeks.

It was among the four shops built by the panchayat next to the community hall in the centre of the village. To begin with, he paid a year's rent and spent another 18,000 rupees to equip it with cheap, locally made television sets and sundry electronic goods. In the following months, Manoj diverted all his earnings towards the rent and managed to pay the panchayat an advance rent for ten years.

*

It was mid March and there was still a chill in the air. Outside the village, acres of lush green wheat crop had just begun to ripen. It would turn golden in a few days, drawing rural Haryana into a centuries-old ritual of harvesting.

Babli called Manoj around noon. It was not the usual mischief but something else that he detected in her voice. 'Come to the dera this evening. Take the road from the scheduled-caste mohalla,' was all she muttered into the phone. He had a load of work to do but his mind kept wandering, thinking about their impending meeting. It was getting increasingly difficult for them to meet, with someone or the other casting knowing glances whenever he went out of his shop nowadays. Babli's mother had also begun piling her with household chores, and for almost a fortnight Babli and he had spoken only for a few minutes each day on the phone. He wondered what was on her mind.

A cool breeze was blowing from the west and there was

still half an hour of daylight left when he reached their usual meeting spot. Ancient mango trees, almost certainly planted by the Nath sadhus, surrounded the dera. Most of them had stopped giving fruit, but on a few of them powdery golden blooms, which would give way to green baby mangoes, had begun to appear. Over the years the trees had grown so high that the fruit did not hold much attraction for the village kids. After hours of pelting stones at them, all they got were a couple of dented mangoes. The villagers left the fruit on the trees for the parrots.

Babli had reached before him. In a mustard salwar kameez, with a maroon dupatta and silver hoops in her ears, she seemed to him like an apsara. As he approached, she rushed to him. A faint odour of cow dung clung to her clothes; clearly, her mother had set her the task of making cow dung cakes that afternoon and she had come straight from the family's barn, which was situated near the pond on the southern side of Karoran. For a long time she did not say anything and Manoj began to get worried. It was not safe for them to be seen at this secluded spot together. Already their families and neighbours had become suspicious and he really didn't want a confrontation. After a long time she lifted her head. 'Do you know what they are planning for me?'

'No. Yes, I mean, are they finding a match for you?' he blurted out his fear. It was something he had been secretly dreading for a long time, though he had never shared this with her. In their social milieu it was logical and inevitable. With her elder sister married at an early age, and Babli forbidden from studying further, she had to be next in line. But, so soon?

'Not finding. Chacha has already found someone. He is from Rohtak, Hooda gotra, with lots of land,' she said with a troubled look on her face. 'They are planning to hold the wedding in October, after paddy harvesting. We have to do something.' He wished he could do something to bring back her smile, but she was disconsolate.

They both knew that no one, not even their mothers or siblings, would approve of their match. The Banwala khap or caste panchayat to which both their families belonged was spread over forty villages around Karoran and never in living memory had anybody married within the same gotra or sub-caste. It was a taboo, punishable by death. They also knew that scores of couples in recent years had paid dearly for lesser offences, like marrying a boy or girl from the same village, even if from different gotras. The khaps also objected to matches between boys and girls of villages that shared a brotherhood pact, called bhaichara. The villages in the Deswali belt of Jats, in which Karoran fell, observed rules of bhaichara whereby any match between them was ordained incestuous. So strict were the rules that even if people from ten gotras lived in a village, all these gotras were taken as belonging to one brotherhood or bhaichara. Matrimonial alliances from any of those ten gotras, across the country, were taboo.

Many months ago Manoj and Babli had decided that come what may they would marry, even if they had to elope. They had been sitting in a park bordering Lake Bidkiyar in Kaithal. It was one of those rare outings when she had found an excuse to go to town with her friends. The friends had been dumped at the bus stand and Manoj had joined her right outside it.

'I will never marry anyone else. I really don't believe in this gotra business. It doesn't make sense in today's world, does it, Manoj?' It was more of a statement than a question. 'If we run away to a big town and marry, it won't bother the khap so much. They won't be able to do much when we are out of their reach. And it won't take long for our relatives to forget it all if they don't see us together as man and wife.'

'We'll cross that bridge when we come to it. Don't spoil this day by worrying about such things,' he had replied.

She had tossed her head, as if she hadn't heard him. 'On television, I've seen so many girls running away to get married. You know, Manoj, it does happen in big towns nowadays, when parents and society don't approve of a love like ours.' Though Manoj did not say much at that time, an unspoken decision had been made.

And today when Ompati told her about the family's decision, Babli had glared at her stone-faced. Her insides shook with rage and despair. As soon as she got a moment to herself, she had quickly dialled Manoj and spent the rest of the day pondering over the problem. After her father's death, she had grown closer to her mother. But something instinctively told her that she could not confide in her about Manoj. Ompati would not have the courage to oppose her Rajinder chacha and other males of the family, she decided. There was Suresh, elder to her by two years, married, with a baby boy. Though they had never been very close, she shared an affection of sorts with him. She, however, dismissed the possibility of any support from his end. Suresh had changed in recent years. She was quite sure he would sing the same tune as Chacha. The family had a good thirty-odd acres of land and was considered one of the influential families in Karoran. Her other chacha, Karambir Singh, was the village sarpanch and had the support of the Congress party. He was the right-hand man of Gangaraj, a powerful Congresswala from their village.

'Oh why can't we live our lives as we please, like people in big towns do? Once we leave Karoran, I will never return to this prison,' she burst out. 'Manoj, do something, or I'll kill myself, if they force me to marry that oaf.' She had begun to cry softly. He had never seen her so helpless. It wasn't like her to become so despondent. Perhaps it was the hopelessness in her voice. Or was it the desperation of their situation? Manoj sensed that things had reached a point of no return. He wiped away her tears and in the gathering darkness of the mango grove they parted.

*

It took a while for Ompati's anger to rise, but once it did even her truculent son Suresh preferred to keep away. This didn't happen very often nowadays. Ever since her husband, Sajjan Singh, had committed suicide a few years ago in a fit of alcohol-induced depression, Ompati had mellowed and readily allowed her brothers-in-law, Rajinder and Karambir, to take major decisions for the family. But that afternoon, as she watched her younger daughter applying kajal to her heavy-lidded eyes and flouncing out of the house in a fetching new blue salwar suit, which she had embroidered herself, Ompati could feel that familiar rage welling up in her. For the last many days she had been hearing whispers of her Babli romping about with that Chandrapati's son, Manoj. Years ago, when she had come as a young bride to Karoran, as part of the post-wedding rituals, out of the many married women of her age in the village, she had chosen Chandrapati as her 'dharam behan', bosom friend. Ompati hardly remembered now, but it was probably on some elderly woman's instructions that she and Chandrapati had tied the sacred red threads on each other's wrists. The friendship continued for many years even though their houses are on opposite ends of the village.

Ompati had married into an influential family of the village; their thirty acres of land ensured that she and her children were comfortably off. Her husband's younger brother, Rajinder Singh, was the head of the family, though the agricultural holdings had been divided between him and Suresh, her eldest son, a few years after her husband's death. Suresh had married a couple of years ago and his year-old son was fast becoming the fulcrum of Ompati's existence. She doted on the mite and even now, as she began shoving sheaves of straw into the fodder-chopping machine, she kept an eye on him, sleeping on a cot in the courtyard. Like in most houses in rural Haryana, in her house too, functionality took precedence over aesthetics. At the entrance was a room where the buffaloes were tethered at night; it also served as a passageway into the courtyard. The fodder-cutting machine, a ubiquitous fixture in agrarian households of North India, occupied centre space.

A crisp blast blew into the house as Suresh pushed open the large wooden door fifteen minutes later. The fresh air lightened the smell of dung and hay which always hung around the entrance, but Ompati hardly noticed the effect.

'This Babli is getting too much. Pandu again told me today that he had seen her going into Manoj's shop. Amma, we'll have to do something,' he burst out, as soon as he saw her.

'I know. But that boy has to be stopped. What guts he has. I can tell that he's the one who is leading Babli astray,' said Ompati as she built up a steady rhythm on the machine. A golden heap of cleanly chopped straw formed on the dung-coated floor. A gust of wind from the open door neatly took off a thin layer from the top and scattered it near the entrance to the courtyard. The flies followed the straw and settled in a corner away from the draught.

'I have half a mind to thrash him one of these days. Will do the same to Babli and they will both come to their senses. Imagine getting involved with a boy from our own gotra! Has she lost her mind?' he growled.

Ompati knew how angry he could get. She swallowed her own anger for a moment to defuse the imminent violence. 'Don't do that. It will aggravate the situation. Better to warn that boy Manoj first. And I will talk to Babli,' she advised.

The next day, Suresh and his friend Pandu discussed the problem in the baithak or sitting room. Rajinder Singh also joined them. Ten minutes later Suresh left for Manoj's shop. The sky was overcast and it seemed as if the unseasonal rain would bring back the February chill for a few days more.

Manoj was running a cold and had a muffler wrapped around his neck, when the two barged into his shop. 'You'd better watch out. If you don't stop communicating with Babli, there will be trouble for you,' Suresh began immediately.

'I am not doing anything. You seem to have a misunderstanding. There is nothing between us,' said the startled Manoj.

But Suresh was in no mood to listen. 'You rat, don't you cross the limits. I am warning you once and for all. Lay off the girl!'

The slightly built Manoj was no match for the tough, muscular Suresh. Suresh was itching to take a swipe at the nervous, blabbering boy, but Manoj did nothing to provoke him. In these parts, discretion is rarely the better part of valour, but it won Manoj a respite that morning. The two stomped out of the shop in disgust.

Manoj was not looking forward to telling his family about Suresh's threat because it would again draw their attention to his growing association with Babli. But he knew the matter had to be discussed. As he had expected, Chandrapati immediately saw red. Rekha and Vinod said very little during the exchange between Manoj and their mother. 'How dare they do this? They think that just because you don't have a father's hand on your head, they can say anything to you? I will take it up with Ompati tomorrow itself,' she said.

Hearing the racket, Seema put away her books and came to the kitchen. 'What are you doing, Manoj? You are fishing in dangerous waters. Ma, you must speak with Babli's mother. We have to put an end to this.'

Manoj was horrified. 'Amma, you will do no such thing. I swear on you, if you go to their house, I will run away from here. You will never see me again. Why are you doing this to me?'

But Chandrapati's blood had begun to boil. She wanted to get even with Babli's family for daring to threaten her Manoj. She hardly listened to his objections. The next morning he again pleaded with her not to go to Babli's house, but as soon as she and Rekha finished cooking the afternoon meal, she took off for their house.

Suresh's wife was massaging Ompati's legs with oil when Chandrapati thundered into their courtyard. 'What do you people think you are? You threatened my Manoj? I swear I will gouge out your eyes if you even cast an evil glance at my son. Put a noose through the nose of your own daughter. She is straying.' She launched a full-blown assault.

Ompati got up at once to defend her daughter. 'You are falsely accusing my Babli. She's not that kind of a girl. I am warning you that if Manoj does not stop phoning her and tries to entice her again, we will call a panchayat. Let them decide what is to be done with him.' It was a short but sharp exchange which was heard in many houses around. Chandrapati was swearing even after she walked out of the doorway. War had been declared between the two families and the first skirmish had just taken place.

*

Manoj had spent a tense day at his shop. The constant chatter of boys who usually hung around the shop irritated him somewhat. He wished his friend Kala, who lived nearby, was here to share his problem, but two days ago Kala had left for Karnal with his parents. He was his closest friend these days and knew all about his relationship with Babli. That ruckus between his mother and Ompati had shaken Manoj and he badly needed to talk to Kala. But Kala returned late at night and wandered into Manoj's shop only the next day. Manoj immediately dropped his screwdriver and took him to the back of the shop. 'Yaar, what you had predicted has happened. The last two days have been so eventful and you were not here to support me,' said Manoj anxiously, as he began to tell his friend about Suresh's threat and the fight between his mother and Ompati.

'The cat is out of the bag, my friend. You'll have to take a decision either way. Back down, or run away and marry her,' Kala said thoughtfully.

'Me and back down? Never! I will show that Suresh what I can do. Once we leave the village, they will not be able to do anything to us. Their might is restricted to the boundaries of Karoran.'

Kala placed his right foot on his left knee and began rubbing the grime off his ankle. Manoj could see that his friend was thinking. For several moments Kala did not speak. He kept rubbing and occasionally brushed aside the grime collecting on the floor. He brought down the right foot, lifted the left one to rub it clean the same way and looked up to speak. 'I know a lawyer in Chandigarh, who once told me that eloping couples from Haryana and Punjab generally head towards Chandigarh as it's easy for them to get married there and get protection from the Punjab and Haryana High Court. I'll talk to him tomorrow.'

'Kala, will you do that for me? You're the only one who supports me in this.' There was relief in Manoj's voice.

It was the 1st of April when Kala finally came to tell him that everything had been fixed for them in Chandigarh. 'A day before you are ready to leave, tell me and I will organize your escape from here,' he said in a low voice. Manoj's heart jumped with fear and elation. The atmosphere at home had become unbearable in the last few days and every day he had to listen to a sermon from Chandrapati on the moral values of their community. Rekha and Vinod were also unhappy at the turn of events and wished their brother would become theirs once again.

Three days elapsed before he could discuss it with Babli. She was delighted. She could hardly wait and wanted to run away that night itself. 'Mother does not let me out of her sight the whole day. And Suresh and Chacha have become so hateful. I don't want to live here any more,' she whispered on the phone.

The next evening when he came home for dinner, he told Chandrapati that he would be sleeping overnight at the shop as he had some work to finish. Babli had promised to reach by 9 p.m. He wondered how she would manage to slip away, as he reached behind a shelf to pull out a small packet containing money that he had been saving all these months. He counted 7600 rupees in soiled notes. Setting aside 5000, he put the notes into his black Rexine wallet; the rest went into the shirt pocket, for ready expenses. By the time Babli arrived, he had locked the shop and was waiting for her in the dark lane which ran between his shop and the community hall. It was the 6th of April.

Her face was flushed and she showed none of the nervousness he was feeling. A light breeze had begun blowing and the road in front of them was dark. The weak crescent of the moon, just three days after amavas, did nothing to light up the street and for once he was glad that there were no street lights on their side of the village. 'I told Ma that I have a tummy ache and want to go to bed early. I hope she doesn't come to check,' she whispered.

He squeezed her hand. Just then Kala joined them and the three walked the short distance to where he had organized an autorickshaw to take them to Kaithal. 'You'd better hurry. Take a night bus to Chandigarh.' Kala handed Manoj the name and telephone number of a person in Chandigarh who would organize the temple wedding for them. 'He specializes in such cases and will organize everything for you. You will have to pay him three thousand five hundred rupees, not more,' he instructed.

They reached Kaithal bus stand just as the last bus to Chandigarh had begun moving out of the enclosure where several other empty buses stood. And it was only when they had bought the tickets and the bus picked up speed that Manoj permitted himself a sigh of relief. Babli was her usual cheerful self and seemed excited about her escape from Karoran. She was humming a tune under her breath and when she found Manoj staring at her she smiled shyly. So absorbed was she in the thrill of what awaited them the next day that the gravity of their situation, and the constant anxiety he was experiencing, eluded her completely. She was so innocent—God, how he wanted to protect and cherish her forever! They were embarking on a new life, bravely walking on an untrodden path and he was daunted by that thought somewhat. 'I will never let any harm befall her,' he resolved.

The bus reached Chandigarh's spacious bus stand at around 3 a.m. Since they had been told to call up their contact at 8 a.m., they wandered towards a dhaba, which was serving aloo parathas to a sprinkling of early-morning travellers like them.

With its extensive gardens, sprawling bungalows enwrapped by foliage, and broad, clean streets, Chandigarh, the joint capital of Punjab and Haryana, is unlike any Indian city. Babli had heard so much about Chandigarh, but this was the first time she had come here and she looked around with interest. At 7.30 a.m. Manoj made the call and he was instructed to reach the Durga Mandir in Sector 56 by 9 a.m. The temple would also give them a certificate to prove that they had got married there.

When they reached the place, they discovered that it was more of a residence and the temple was a small room with pictures of gods and goddesses. The pundit seemed to be an expert at marrying off eloping couples and was ready with marigold garlands in a brown paper bag for them. He quickly lighted a fire in an iron brazier, threw some incense into it and asked Manoj and Babli to exchange the garlands. She slipped on some red bangles which they had bought from the Sector 22 rehri market, and Manoj solemnly filled her hair-parting with sindoor. Fifteen minutes later, they were man and wife. All this while, the pundit's assistant had been taking their pictures and finally he asked them to pose together with the garlands round their necks. Manoj in his bright blue T-shirt and Babli in a red kurta and black tie-and-dye dupatta looked radiant, as they smiled shyly into the camera.

*

That Manoj did not sleep in his shop the night he had fled with Babli for Chandigarh became known only later. At home, the next morning, Chandrapati had waited for him to return from the shop and go to Cheeka, the subdivision town some thirty-five kilometres away, where he was to take his Plus Two compartment exams that day. She hurried to make an early breakfast for him and wondered why he was late in coming. 'I hope he hasn't overslept. He won't get a bus to take him to Cheeka in time,' she fretted. Just then there was a knock on the door and a young man came in. They would later learn he was Gurdev, Babli's cousin from her maternal side, who lived in Jakhauli village.

'Where is Manoj?' were his first words.

Chandrapati looked surprised and asked, 'What work do you have with him?'

'He owes me some money and I have come to take it back.'

'When did he borrow it?'

Gurdev stood with his hands on his hips in the courtyard and replied, 'He took it some time ago and I need the money now.'

'You sit and have some tea. Manoj will be here shortly,' she said, somewhat uneasily.

Their early-morning visitor chatted over tea, inquiring about their family and what the children were doing. Still there was no sign of Manoj. Gurdev's attitude changed completely. Turning towards Chandrapati, he said, 'Your Manoj has run away with our girl. They have been missing since last night. Either you tell us where they are or things will get worse for you all.'

His words struck them like a bolt of lightning. Chandrapati paled and, for a moment, was at a loss for words. Seema responded, 'Listen, we don't know what you are talking about. Manoj has to give his exam at Cheeka today, and will be here soon.'

Now that he had revealed the real purpose of his visit, Gurdev continued in the same vein. 'We had warned him not to do anything rash. He will have to pay for it.'

The two women tried to protest, but Gurdev had delivered his message and, with an angry flourish and a parting

'We'll hound him and you till the ends of the earth', walked out of the door.

For a while, they sat in stunned silence. Then Seema and Vinod left the house to check at Manoj's shop. 'Has he really run away? Is that why he hasn't turned up for breakfast till now?' they wondered. Seema found the door of the shop locked and no trace of Manoj anywhere.

Around mid morning a group of people from the village landed at their door. 'Bhai dekh Chandrapati, you'd better come clean and tell us where that Manoj of yours has hidden Babli. He has brought shame on the entire village and you will all have to bear the consequence of his actions,' said one of them.

The next day, another group, calling themselves members of the khap panchayat, came up and forcefully demanded to know the whereabouts of Manoj. No one was prepared to believe that they didn't know where he was. 'No telephone call, no contact number. His phone is switched off. We have no knowledge,' Seema repeated ad nauseam to the never-ending groups of ponderous panchayats that trooped into their house morning and evening over the next few days. They banged on their door at odd hours; sometimes two or more groups came to the house in a day to issue threats.

By now Chandrapati was out of her mind with worry and wondered if Babli's relatives had kidnapped her son to pressurize him to break off his relationship with Babli. About a week after Manoj went missing, she decided to lodge an FIR at their local police station at Rajaund and on 14 April she and Seema went there. By now the news of the couple's disappearance had spread all around and the police too were aware of the events in Karoran village. The policemen told Chandrapati, 'It is your son who has kidnapped the girl. We cannot lodge your complaint.'

Seema thought they hadn't understood what Chandrapati was trying to say. 'Ma, you can't even explain a simple thing like this. Let me handle this,' she said, and edged ahead of her mother to repeat it all over again. She argued long and hard but they were unmoved. They went again, on 24 April, this time accompanied by Manoj's cousin Narinder, but the Rajaund police seemed determined not to lodge Chandrapati's FIR. Seema sensed something was amiss, but she couldn't put her finger on it straight away.

Two days later, on 26 April, the very same policemen of Rajaund police station, who had refused to entertain Chandrapati's complaint, booked her instead for colluding with her son Manoj to kidnap Babli. Among the accused were Seema and three of Manoj's friends from the village. The FIR was lodged by Babli's influential family, with Ompati as the complainant, and almost immediately the police swung into action. Ompati's complaint gave Babli's age as seventeen years (a minor), and it is a matter of record that no one at the police station bothered to verify if this was indeed true. No birth or school-leaving certificate accompanied the FIR. It was a small detail but its significance eluded Chandrapati and Seema until many months later.

Some days the police would summon Chandrapati and Seema to the police station, where Head Constable Jai Inder Singh, the SHO Jagbir Singh and a lady constable questioned them. Sometimes they would be made to wait the entire day at the police station before the policemen even attended to them. Chandrapati was at her wits' end and, when it appeared that the Rajaund police might arrest her to placate the complainants, Narinder and Mahavir Singh, her husband's friend, advised her to seek anticipatory bail from the Kaithal sessions court. They helped her to draft a petition for the court and on 5 May she was granted anticipatory bail. But the court asked her to cooperate with the police in its investigation and present herself when required. That provided some respite from the fear of impending arrest.

Nonetheless, a few khap leaders got into a car and took off for SHO Jagbir Singh's house in Jind to persuade him to arrest Chandrapati. When he told them that she had been given anticipatory bail and it would not be possible for him to arrest her, they were undeterred. An insinuation that the SHO was not arresting Chandrapati because he had taken a shine to Seema began doing the rounds in Karoran. It reached the intended target—Seema—a couple of days later.

She learned of it from a friend while walking home from the corner grocery shop. 'Seema, the village is buzzing with rumours about your alleged relationship with the SHO. Be careful,' she said as they neared their homes. Seema was by now getting used to the sustained onslaught on them, but she had not anticipated this. She later told herself that she should have been prepared for something like this, a below-the-belt assault. Such assaults on strong women were common in that milieu but for Seema this was a first. The first of many more to come. She didn't know whether to alert Chandrapati or to just let it be and hope her mother did not hear of it from anyone else. So far Chandrapati had handled the pressure well and the last thing Seema wanted was to burden her with more.

Dipping into her emotional reserves to cope with this one, she went to bed troubled. Tomorrow would be another day.

*

When the celebrated French architect Le Corbusier designed Chandigarh in the early 1960s, he retained the villages whose lands were acquired for this showpiece city, as semi-rural islands dotting the precise, linear cityscape. Many of the elite who live in Chandigarh today find them an eyesore and wish Corbusier had eliminated them on the drawing board itself. Villages like Dadu Majra, Attawa, Hallo Majra and many more, with their cattle and dung, higgledy-piggledy shops and stinking open drains, exist within Chandigarh's sanitized boundaries. It was to one such village, Burail, that Manoj and Babli headed to for a room to rent, when they began running out of money towards the end of April 2007.

They had been married for almost a month and, from what Manoj had learned from his friends back in Karoran, the situation was still very tense. There was no question of their going back for some time at least. He had managed to get a job with a travel agency, which paid him 2500 rupees a month. They rented a room for 500 rupees a month and set up home there. It was a modest single-storey building which housed a few other tenants like them. Their little home accorded them some stability and, with Manoj's job bringing in a little money, they were getting by. But Manoj had still not called up his mother and knew that she, Seema, Rekha and Vinod were facing the music after his elopement. It was not possible to put off contacting them. He wanted to talk to them, was even missing them a little. So one evening after he returned from work, he dialled the number of his home back in Karoran. A nervous Babli sat close to him.

Manoj's call put life back into his mother. Chandrapati was so relieved to hear from him that she forgot her anger and fears, forgot to berate him for putting them through the agony of the last few weeks, or for breaking the social taboos of their clan. She was hearing his voice after more than a month. 'Amma, it's me, Manoj. I am well and in

Chandigarh with Babli. We are married,' he said in a quiet voice. It was the middle of May.

'Beta, I hope you are all right. We are happy that you have married Babli, but be careful of her relatives. They are searching for you like hounds. I will come to meet you both as soon as I can,' she gushed into the phone. Her darling Manoj had surfaced. She immediately headed for the two pictures of Ram and Sita and one of Lord Krishna which were kept in a small alcove in the inner room. This was her small shrine at home. 'Hey Bhagwan, I am so thankful to you for this mercy. Please protect my children, let no harm befall them,' she murmured, as she lit incense and rubbed her forehead on the holy shelf. The tears fell unbidden.

They began planning to go to Chandigarh to meet Manoj and his bride almost immediately. Chandrapati toyed with the idea of gifting Babli the two gold bangles she herself had got married in, but then abandoned the thought. She would give them to Babli whenever she came home, she thought. They bought a pair of anklets, some artificial jewellery and new clothes for the bride and, three days after hearing from him, Seema and Chandrapati set off for Chandigarh to meet the couple.

They seemed happy. Babli had covered her head and touched Chandrapati's feet when she entered. Though Chandrapati felt a cut of resentment at the troubles which had befallen them because of this girl, she suppressed her feelings and stretched out her hand to bless her daughter-in-law. Babli made tea for everybody and they caught up with the events of the past month. Despite Manoj's job, the two seemed desperately short of money and Babli told them that there were days when they had to make do with just one meal. The little money that they had fled with had not lasted long and most of it had been spent on lodging in cheap guest houses and eating at dhabas.

Manoj seemed well aware of the commotion in Karoran after their disappearance. Even though he had not called them, he had been keeping in touch with his friends in the village, who had given him all the news. Chandrapati was categorical that they should not come anywhere near the village till the matter had cooled down. 'They will make a noise for a few weeks and will eventually have to forget it all. The important thing is to keep out of sight and not show yourself,' she advised them.

Seema chatted with Babli and the two girls were getting to know each other. She liked what she saw of her sister-in-law and perhaps for the first time began to understand why Manoj had done what he had. At one stage, Seema asked her, 'Aren't you missing your home, Babli?'

Then Babli, all of nineteen years, turned serious and said, 'Not much, but I wish I could meet my ma. How is she? I wonder what she is going through . . .'

Seema could not tell her much. Babli's family members had hounded them so much in the last few days, but there was never a word from Ompati. It was as if she had withdrawn into herself. Seema did, however, tell her about the fury of Suresh and her cousins, and their frenzied search for her and Manoj.

Babli's eyes filled with tears. 'They can never give me the happiness that I wanted. Manoj and I do not have much money here, but we are content. I could not breathe in that house. Suresh used to beat me . . .'

They were two happy women who walked back from the bus stop on the outskirts of Karoran, towards their small house that evening. Mother and daughter carrying a bag of vegetables, an empty nylon bag and plenty of smiles. After days of uncertainty they had found something to be happy about and they hurried home to tell Vinod and Rekha about their trip to Chandigarh. It was the simple joy of welcoming a new member into their family. In the event, her becoming a mother-in-law would turn out to have far-reaching consequences for Chandrapati. Far more than she could ever have imagined.

PART TWO

The Aftermath

Chapter Three

'The Bodies Are Here'

There is nothing to distinguish modern-day Kaithal from scores of dusty, garbage-strewn mofussil towns of North India. The chaotic traffic, honking buses that bully cyclists and pedestrians, and a collapsing civic infrastructure add to the inhabitants' daily woes. The town even has a locality called Ganda Nallah Wali Gali or 'the alley by the sewage gutter'. Little wonder few townspeople even care that Kaithal is regarded as the birthplace of Hanuman. There is a temple dedicated to him at Anjani ka Tila (Anjani was Hanuman's mother), a mound at the town's edge. Kaithal, though, is said to have been founded by Yudhishtra, the wise Pandava king of the Mahabharata, to commemorate his victory over the Kauravas. He named it Kapisthala, Sanskrit for 'abode of monkeys', for its association with Hanuman. In 1989 Kaithal became the district headquarters, bounded by Kurukshetra on the north, Karnal on the east and Jind district on the south.

Criss-crossed with canals from the rivers Sutlej and Yamuna, Kaithal district has bumper rice and wheat crops year after year. It benefitted hugely from the Green Revolution and even today farmers here practise multi-cropping and rarely leave their fields fallow for more than a month.

Karoran is one of the larger villages in Kaithal district with a population of almost 25,000. With around 10,000 voters, it is eyed by politicians of all hues, who are always looking for ways of making it their pocket borough. Like many other villages of Kaithal and Kurukshetra districts, Karoran is said to have a rich past, replete with legends and temples. It is named after Kaundiya rishi, who is believed to have meditated by the sacred pond there. The Kaithili Brahmin who founded the village named it Kodan, and there is a temple at the spot where he established a khera (the first settlement). Karoran also has a sati temple, dedicated to an unknown woman who became a sati here. Such women are still revered in Haryana and Rajasthan, though the practice of sati was banned in the nineteenth century.

The land is steeped in religion, mythology and lore. Here old and new social mores often clash with brutal consequences; here people like Manoj and Babli have to die at the altar of community honour. Only then can order be restored in society.

15 June

It was almost 9 p.m. and dark as sin when the deed was done. What remained was to dispose of the bodies. The men unanimously decided that they should be thrown into the Sirsa branch canal some fifty kilometres away. Rajinder felt it was sufficiently far from Karoran and the current would carry the bodies further downstream. That was how it appeared and remained in the official records, which reconstructed the event many months later.

1.30 a.m., 16 June

Seema's head throbbed. They had been up half the night desperately calling on Manoj's mobile number: 92555-21766; Chandrapati and she tried it again and again. All they got was a bland pre-recorded voice message saying the phone was switched off. Since his call from the STD booth in Pipli the previous afternoon, there had been no word from Manoj or Babli. Chandrapati was sick with worry after hearing about Babli's relatives following them. She had not been able to eat. Rekha had taken over the cutting of fodder on the small hand-turned machine the previous evening. She filled up the feeding troughs of their three buffaloes and came back inside to sit beside Seema, who was working the phone in vain. Vinod, a year younger than her, was pacing restlessly between the handpump and the entrance to the courtyard. So weighed down were they with anxiety that they completely missed the eerie silence in the village that night.

It was as if the village had retired early. There was none of the chatter of women washing utensils after dinner or the chit-chat in dark lanes as they took their children out to defecate at the stinking drains running along the outer walls of houses. Their own lane was deathly quiet and no one dropped by that evening to chat or exchange a katori of dal. But a large group of grizzled old men sat talking on charpoys in the village chaupal till late in the night, as they passed the hookah around. Some men also clustered under the few street lights in the village murmuring. They seemed in no hurry to go home to their wives that night.

Dawn broke bright and clear. There was still no word from Manoj. Seema and Vinod went to check on Manoj's shop and to bring home anything of value, to keep it safe. The events of the previous day had so completely unnerved the family that, unconsciously, they had begun to roll back in defence. Even as they walked to the shop, a short distance from their home, Seema was constantly dialling Manoj's number, hoping against hope that he would take the call. On the way back, they bumped into Paro, their neighbour, taking the buffaloes to the village pond for their daily bath. Seema smiled at her, but Paro avoided looking at them and, cracking her stick on the buffalo nearest to her, quickly herded them on. 'What's wrong with her?' Seema wondered for a moment before the more pressing matter of Manoj's whereabouts pushed the thought out.

'Ma, the shop is okay. We have brought back two television sets and a tape recorder and put the big lock on the door,' she announced as she walked into their mud-plastered courtyard.

'Seema, you get ready quickly. We are going to the Rajaund thana to find out about Manoj,' said a troubled Chandrapati.

Before she could reply, Vinod piped up, 'What will they tell us, Ma? You know that even if they have any information about Manoj, they will first tell Babli's relatives. They are not with us. Nobody is.'

But Chandrapati was already pulling out a fresh salwar suit from the trunk kept in the inner room. 'Our village falls under the jurisdiction of Rajaund thana. The court had ordered them to provide security to Manoj and Babli. They should know where they are and whether they are safe. We will have to go to them. If they don't respond, then I will meet SP sahib at Kaithal.' The two left without touching the chapattis and tea Rekha had made for them.

Chandrapati's husband died in 1991 and, in the years that followed, the family had seen three deaths. Her father-in-law, Hari Singh, who had shouldered the family responsibilities for much of his life, passed away in 1997.

After the old man's death, Satbir's younger brother Bhim Singh took on the mantle of the family patriarch, but a year later he too died of a debilitating illness. His wife died in 2005 in a road accident. Their closest relatives during those days, then, were Bhim Singh's two sons, Narinder and Vicky, both of whom were infrequent visitors to Karoran as they were working in Chandigarh and Kurukshetra respectively. On that day, it fell on the delicate, innocent twenty-year-old Seema and her mother to make the lonely journey to the police station.

Rajaund is a sub-tehsil of Kaithal district. The police station was housed in a crumbling building, with walls damp and swollen from seepage and spattered with moss. A miniature forest of grass and peepul plants had sprouted from the roof and sometimes, when the policemen slammed the termite-eaten doors shut, they came off their hinges. For the last few years, pending the shift of the police station to a new building, maintenance funds had been stopped, and the policemen were condemned to these dark and dank rooms.

When Chandrapati went up to them, as Vinod had predicted, the policemen expressed their inability to help. 'We have no information about them. We left them at Pipli and they were to take a bus to Delhi from there,' said SI Jagbir Singh, when Chandrapati queried him.

'Yes, he called me from an STD booth at Pipli. But you were to provide them protection till their destination, weren't you?' she persisted.

At this, the SI pulled out two papers from a grubby drawer under his table. They had been signed by Manoj and Babli the day before, when the police party had left them at Pipli. The two almost identical statements said that they had got married in a temple in Chandigarh and Babli had given a statement before the magistrate under Section 164 of the CrPc that she had married Manoj of her own will and wanted to live with him as his wife. The operative words that Seema immediately picked out were: 'I have no need of police protection, and whenever I come into this area and need the security, I will ask for it.' The two statements bore the signatures of Head Constable Dharampal and constables Usha Rani and Satbir Singh, from the protection party, as witnesses. Defeated, Chandrapati and Seema walked out of the gloomy police station and took a bus back to Karoran. Seema felt as if the men in khaki, far from even pretending to be helpful, were smirking at them.

Meanwhile, a reporter with *Dainik Bhaskar* based in Kaithal, who had been following the Manoj–Babli kidnapping case, received a call around noon from one of his sources in Karoran. 'The bodies of Manoj and Babli are in the village, at this very moment,' his source informed him. The reporter made a quick call to Narinder, who had a clerical job in the Haryana State Electricity department, to check if this was true. Utterly puzzled, Narinder replied, 'I don't think that is possible. I haven't heard anything to that effect.' The reporter dropped the story but Narinder grew alert. After smoke, even if a wisp, there had to be fire. But where?

17 June

There was an air of utter despondency in the Chandrapati household. They knew that it wasn't like Manoj to be incommunicado for so long. He had not called them up for about a month immediately after his marriage, fearing a verbal whiplash from his mother, but the family knew that even during those days he had kept himself informed about their well-being through contact with his close friends in the village.

But with no help forthcoming from the police and Babli's powerful family assuming threatening postures, it was time to seek help from their relatives. 'Where had the two vanished? Had they met with an accident? Were they being held captive by Babli's brothers? Oh God, what if . . .' The thoughts raced through Chandrapati's mind.

Seema once again began working the phones and the first call was to her cousin Narinder. She then called his younger brother, Vicky, at Kurukshetra, her maternal uncle, paternal aunt and several other relatives scattered in nearby villages.

Narinder immediately took a week's leave and boarded the afternoon bus for Karoran. Her father's friend Mahavir Singh from Jind was the only other one who responded. Many years ago, when Chandrapati and her husband lived in Delhi Cantonment for a couple of years, Narinder had stayed with them. This was before she had her own children and she had come to look upon him as her own. The bond strengthened in the years following the death of his parents and now they are like one family.

By the time Narinder walked into their dimly lit courtyard late that evening, the family had all but given up hope. They had received a disturbing piece of news. A nervous neighbour had dropped in that afternoon to say that an informal panchayat had been called by some people in the village where it was announced, *'Kaam ho gaya'*—the deed has been done. Those who had gathered nodded in satisfaction. The family was devastated by the thought that, even as they had been calling Manoj's number in vain and pleading with the Rajaund police for some information about him, such an announcement had been made in the village. 'They killed them in Suresh's fields. Many people from the village saw them doing it. Chandrapati, it's all over. You must forget him,' said their neighbour by way of offering condolences. Chandrapati wanted to slap her hand over the woman's mouth and push her out of the house for uttering this profanity. She didn't believe a word of what she had heard. Instead, she began pounding the bajra grains in the stone mortar in the corner of the veranda for the evening meal of khichdi. Right next to the mortar was a small grinding stone which Vinod operated on weekends to make atta for rotis. She pounded the grain with vengeance. For more than an hour, without uttering a word. Just the rhythmic sound of the wooden pestle hitting the fine grains. Seema and Rekha watched their mother silently from the kitchen window.

Vinod had gone out to meet a friend and brought similar news on his return. 'The whole village is discussing the deaths, Ma. They could not have killed them just like that. It must be a rumour, a lie,' he said, as he tried to play down the horror. In their heart of hearts, the four feared the worst but no one dared to mention it. Even now, neither Chandrapati nor Seema was prepared to believe the rumours until they had definite proof. They pinned their hopes on Narinder. Though just thirty-five, he was the head of their family by virtue of being the oldest surviving male member. Manoj was a good twelve years younger but they resembled each other, having inherited the features and frame of their paternal side. Villagers often said that they could pass for real brothers.

Narinder had spent the day contacting his friends in Kaithal and surrounding villages and he too had picked up the same news from them. Not wanting to alarm them further, he kept what he had learned to himself. To Chandrapati, he said, 'Taayi, you don't worry. First thing tomorrow morning, I will set out to search for them myself.'

18 June

Narinder's first stop was the STD booth at Pipli from where Manoj had last called his mother three days ago. He showed the picture of Manoj and Babli, which Seema had given him in the morning, to Vijay Kumar, the owner of the STD booth at Parakeet. It was taken on the day of their marriage and they were wearing marigold garlands round their necks. Vijay immediately remembered the nervous couple and had no problem identifying them from the picture. He told Narinder that they had taken a Karnal-bound bus.

Then Narinder undertook the tedious task of stopping at every police station that fell between Pipli and Karnal. Some eighteen kilometres short of the district headquarters of Karnal, at a police station in the small town of Butana, he got his first lead: policemen there told him that they had received a call for assistance regarding a kidnapping on the 15th evening from the toll plaza near Arjaheri village. Arjaheri is two and a half kilometres from Butana and comes within its beat. The Butana policemen gave Narinder the telephone number of the caller, Kuldeep, the contractor at the toll plaza who had witnessed the abduction. He rushed to the toll plaza. On seeing the picture of Manoj and Babli, Kuldeep immediately recognized the duo and confirmed that they had indeed been kidnapped by around ten men in a Scorpio on the 15th. He also produced Manoj's shoe, which had fallen off during the struggle, and described to Narinder the entire sequence as he had witnessed it that horrible afternoon. Narinder's heart sank. He realized at once that it was all over. It was now just a question of finding the bodies. But when he called Seema an hour later he did not voice these thoughts. He said, instead, 'Seema, tell Taayi that I have some information. I think we will be able to find them soon. Will tell you more when I come back in the evening.'

19 June

The gloom in the house deepened after what Narinder told them on his return. None of them had slept well and Seema could hear Rekha sobbing into her pillow late into the night. Overwhelmed by the distressing news they had got over the last two days, Seema had no strength left to comfort her little sister. They lay there restless, suffering in their own cocoons.

Early in the morning they collected in the courtyard veranda to decide what to do next. Narinder suggested that they should go once more to Rajaund police station to register an FIR of kidnapping and abduction against Babli's relatives, since they had proof of the kidnapping now. Chandrapati seconded this resolutely. 'We can't keep sitting helplessly like this. These dogs have done something to my Manoj, I know. We have to do something.'

Quiet and tense, the trio of Narinder, Chandrapati and Seema made their way to the bus stop on the outskirts of Karoran, from where they caught a bus for Rajaund. Lost in their respective thoughts, they said little to each other, as they walked through the dung-spattered village lanes. The villagers fell silent when they passed by and no one made an attempt to talk to them.

Once again, the Rajaund police declined to help. 'We have come to know that our boy Manoj and his wife, Babli, have been abducted near Nilokheri in Karnal. It's been executed by Babli's brother and cousins and we have come to register an FIR against them,' said Narinder.

As Chandrapati opened her mouth to speak, tears stung her eyes. Tears that had turned to stone now brimmed over, threatening to dent her composure. She pulled herself together and, injecting her voice with a firmness she did not feel, said, 'I fear that they have been killed and want you to investigate the matter and take appropriate action.'

SI Jagbir heard them out, but made no effort to heed their request. He instead suggested that they should try their luck at the office of the senior superintendent of police (SSP) at Kaithal. 'You will have to meet SSP sahib for this. I can't help you,' he told them in an expressionless voice. Behind their backs, Head Constable Dharampal and Head Constable Jai Inder Singh looked at each other and smiled.

They caught a bus to Kaithal, some thirty kilometres away, and reached the SSP's office, the district police headquarters, by late afternoon. He was away for a meeting and they decided to wait for him. They hung around the office complex till it was time for offices to close but there was still no sign of him. Chandrapati was determined not to leave without meeting him. Eventually, Narinder went into the room adjacent to the SSP's office, which was presided over by his private secretary. A couple of policemen standing around the small room drew in to listen. They were all of the opinion that since the abduction had taken place in an area under the jurisdiction of Butana police station, the FIR would only be registered there. 'You are wasting your time here, SSP sahib will not be able to do much,' they told him.

By the time they came out of the office complex it was late and they realized that there was no point in going back to Karoran for the night. Staying the night with relatives in Kaithal was out of the question, because no relative would welcome them in. So it was to a dharamsala that they headed for the night and the next morning they took a bus for Butana.

20 June

Mahavir Singh was waiting for them at Butana police station and Seema felt better there was one more in their group. She was due to go back to Jaipur that very day. She had an exam the next day. It was the last thing on her mind, but she had decided to sit for the exam anyway. The law degree that she had been pursuing in Jaipur for the last two years was important for her. She planned to catch a bus for Jaipur after they were done at Butana. 'The cops here might listen to us. They are not influenced by Babli's family,' she thought.

Butana police station was housed in a reasonably well-maintained building, but Chandrapati and Narinder found that the attitude of the policemen here was just as unhelpful. They told Narinder that he had come to the wrong place and that he would have to go to Kaithal to file an FIR. This in spite of the call they had received five days ago regarding an abduction in their area. But by now Narinder was better prepared. He decided to call the few local journalists from the Haryanavi print and electronic media whose contact numbers he was armed with. He knew that the news of the kidnapping of Manoj and Babli from the toll plaza had been picked up by local newspapers in the last two days and that reporters would be keen to chase the story. Within the hour they descended on the police station and, once Narinder had briefed them about the matter, they took over. Ultimately, Assistant Sub-Inspector Dharampal Singh registered an FIR under Section 364 of the Indian Penal Code (IPC) with Chandrapati as the complainant. Her apprehension that her son and daughter-in-law had been abducted with the intention of killing them was duly recorded. The names of the suspects were given as Suresh,

Babli's brother; Rajinder Singh, her chacha; and Gurdev Singh, her cousin; besides others.

*

Chandrapati and Narinder returned to Karoran with some hope in their hearts that the abductors of Manoj and Babli would be punished. But both knew that there was little chance of finding them alive.

It was most certainly the presence of the media at the police station in Butana that spurred the cops there into immediate action. By evening, the cops had interrogated Kuldeep at the toll plaza, taken the blue-and-white shoe belonging to Manoj into custody and reached Karoran to arrest the accused. A couple of cops from Rajaund police station also accompanied them. As soon as the Gypsy bearing the policemen approached Ompati's house, the news spread like wildfire in the village and groups of men armed with stones and lathis turned out to send them away. The police party did, however, manage to pick up Suresh's younger brother Kala, and beat a quick retreat. Within the hour, tractor trolleys full of angry men from Karoran descended on Rajaund police station. They came armed with lathis and farm implements. The policemen did not offer any resistance and, as one participant later noted, 'It was as if they were waiting for someone to come and take the boy from them. They didn't seem to know what to do with him. He wasn't one of the accused in the FIR.'

The abductors of Manoj and Babli and their supporters in Karoran were enraged that Chandrapati had dared to register a case against them.

21 June

It was around mid morning when Seema asked Vinod to get her cell phone recharged from the shop nearby. With all the calls she had made in the last two days, the balance was nil. Vinod jumped at the opportunity to get out of the house. His mother had handed him a small list of groceries she needed and he planned to drop by his classmate Rakesh's house on the way back, to pick up some more news. As he approached their usual corner shop, he saw a crowd of men dispersing from the aasan, the open ground with a platform where people traditionally assembled for the panchayat and where major decisions were taken. As he handed his phone for a recharge the man in the shop turned him away. Vinod was puzzled. 'What's the matter? Is your system not working today?'

'Don't you know?' he replied curtly. 'That panchayat breaking up just now was to discuss your family. It has issued a fatwa for the village to socially and economically boycott all of you. Go away, no one will sell you anything.' It was the same story at the corner grocery shop. Somewhat disconcerted but still not alarmed, the boy hurried home to convey the news of this latest assault on them. Strangely, no one had bothered to inform them about the convening of this meeting. The whole village seemed to have been present there, besides a horde of television and print journalists from Kaithal. It was a decision made by the powerful people of the village. No one even wanted to bother with going through the motions of hearing their defence.

The family was left dismayed and shocked. 'What is our crime? They have abducted our children and possibly killed them too and, instead of them being punished, the villagers are punishing us!' Chandrapati voiced the thoughts of everyone around her.

That morning, the aasan situated right opposite Karoran's ancient temples had been a sea of white kurta pyjamas and turbans. Men and boys of all shapes and sizes had rallied there, surcharged. The womenfolk as usual had to be content with whatever they could see of the happenings from the rooftops or windows of their houses. The Banwala khap had decreed that since Manoj had brought disrepute to the clan by having an incestuous relationship with a girl from the same gotra and the same village, who in the eyes of the community was his sister, his family would have to face the consequences. It was made clear that they had earned the wrath of the community only because they had dared to file a police case against its respected members. The boycott would also extend to their relatives in Chandigarh and Kurukshetra, that is, Narinder and Vicky.

The star of the event was indisputably the handsome, imposing Gangaraj. Tall and well built, with a raised nose and smattering of grey in his thick hair, he made a sharp impression in his sparkling white shirt and pyjama. Whenever people spoke about him, it was in slight awe—that he was a Congress activist, very influential, knew a number of ministers. Today, though, he was speaking as a senior member of the Banwala khap, holding forth for the benefit of the television cameras that video-recorded the event.

Gangaraj asserted that marrying within the gotra was against kinship norms and the boycott was ordered because they had lost their girl and, on top of it, the boy's mother had filed a false case against some members of the community and the girl's family. They would have to withdraw the case. Anyone who talked to them, had business or any other dealings with them would be fined 25,000 rupees and be subject to the boycott as well.

Word about the fatwa spread to the surrounding villages

before the day was done. It's hard to say whether it was the horror of the brutal murders, the brazenness of the perpetrators, the display of their might, or all of these which silenced the dissenters. And there were many of them in Karoran that day but none dared to speak up in defence of Chandrapati's family.

23 June

The dead bodies of Manoj and Babli were fished out of the Balsamand Minor canal near Narnaund in Hisar district from two separate places, Sandlana and Kheri Chopta. The bodies had surfaced due to the stoppage of water in the canal. But Narnaund is more than a hundred kilometres from Karoran and the policemen there did not connect the discovery with the kidnapping incident which had taken place on 15 June at the Karnal toll plaza. If the Rajaund police appeared to have been complicit, the policemen at Narnaund came across as grossly negligent.

Three days earlier, on 20 June, after Chandrapati's FIR regarding the kidnapping of her son and daughter-in-law had been registered by the Butana police, a verbal transmission (VT) message had been sent to all police stations in Haryana. The message was based on her complaint of abduction and stated that any police station that received information about the whereabouts of the two was to inform the Butana police. The VT message had been received and recorded by the Narnaund police but it rang no bell when the two bodies were recovered from their area. They did not think it necessary to inform the Butana police about this and sent the bodies to the Post Graduate Institute of Medical Sciences (PGIMS) at Rohtak for a post-mortem the same day. The bodies of Manoj and Babli were cremated as unclaimed bodies the next day, even as a manhunt was on in the state to find them. The police did, however, keep the clothes worn by the two, some jewellery found on Babli's body, the ropes around their bodies and the sack used to wrap Manoj. The Narnaund police then issued a VT message of its own, informing all police stations in Haryana that two bodies of a male and a female with ropes binding their limbs had been recovered from the Balsamand canal falling in their area. If any thana had a complaint about a missing couple, they were to inform the Narnaund police! The ingenuity of some in the Haryana police is remarkable. All it takes is a few taps on the transmitter and the responsibility of investigating a tedious matter is conveniently shifted.

In Karoran, meanwhile, murmurs about the disposal of Manoj's and Babli's bodies were growing louder. They offered some explanation for the discovery more than a hundred kilometres away, in a canal that did not pass near the village, and Narinder had kept his antennae tuned for more information, ever since he had received the call from the *Dainik Bhaskar* reporter on 16 June. Like in any village elsewhere, nothing escapes the local grapevine—the goings-on in households, the enmities, the furtive love affairs and who stole whose share of canal water. Tapping into this source that in his experience was possibly closest to the truth, Narinder pieced together a plausible account. Chandrapati also heard a similar account from well-wishers, almost a week later, and it made her heart sink. The gory details of how the two were brutally killed and their bodies thrown into the canal rent her heart. Slowly, more details about who all were present from the village, some even from their own lane, in Suresh's fields, watching or assisting the killings, surfaced. Until then, after Narinder had returned from Pipli, she had believed that the two had only been abducted.

The village rumour mill churned for weeks and in each retelling the account got embellished. The story that the family finally pieced together went like this: The bodies of the ill-fated couple were thrown in the Minor canal which passes by Mundhal and Bakal, two neighbouring villages. But due to the stoppage of water in the canal, the bodies were spotted by some villagers in Bakal who informed the police.

Babli's family also received the information that the bodies had surfaced. They were then taken on a buffalo cart to Karoran and kept there for some hours. The policemen from Rajaund police station came in an official vehicle and helped Babli's relatives transport the bodies to the larger Sirsa branch canal, some sixty kilometres from Karoran, where they were finally dumped.

Chandrapati wailed and swore within the confines of her room, her rage overflowing. 'May the future generations of these animals be destroyed! May the wombs of their women decay and turn barren! They have conspired and killed my Manoj so heartlessly. And, oh Lord, even as I was searching for him like a madwoman, they brought his body here. Oh, why did someone not tell me then? At least I could have seen his face.'

It was many weeks later that the family summoned the courage to tell people outside Karoran what they had learned about the actual end of Manoj and Babli. One of them was the SP Crime at Karnal who received an unpublicized complaint from Chandrapati. This is what her complaint said:

> There are rumours in the village that on 15/06/07 after killing Manoj and Babli their bodies were thrown into a minor canal near Bakal and Mundhal villages. At night, due to stoppage of water in the canal, their

> bodies got stuck on the bed, where they were spotted by someone from Mundhal the next morning. The information about the two bodies was conveyed to Sub-Inspector Jagbir Singh of Rajaund Thana who then, with the help of Babli's relatives, got them thrown further away, in the Sirsa branch canal. In return for this, the SI took Rs 8 lakh from them.

Her complaint also lists the names of at least ten more people who, according to her, were present and witnessed the killings. She doesn't know what became of it, or whether anyone investigated the additional inputs provided by her. In Karoran, her version of the story still holds.

*

A small resistance movement had begun to take shape in the village. Narinder was sitting in Manoj's shop, mulling over the social boycott and its implications on their day-to-day life, when a friend stopped by to invite him for a meeting. He was surprised to find twenty-odd young men from their locality gathered in his friend's baithak.

'Come, Narinder. We have gathered here to discuss the boycott call given by the panchayat against your family,' said Krishan.

The harried Narinder wondered if this wasn't yet another stratagem to humiliate his family. The last two days had been hell. No one from the village was ready to sell them milk and he had had to buy a packet of milk powder from nearby Pundri. That very morning, a worried Seema had told him that the person from whom they had contracted to buy fodder for the year had returned the 6000-rupee advance she had given him a few days earlier, saying he could no longer sell them fodder. They could not hire any private autorickshaw or cab to go from Karoran to Rajaund or elsewhere. The auto drivers averted their eyes when any of them approached. One of them did agree to take them to Rajaund but demanded double the fare. They were forced to rely on the infrequent and often erratic roadways buses. A sense of being abandoned and isolated began to settle upon them.

Narinder looked hesitantly at the faces gathered in the baithak. Among the boys who had called him for the meeting were some of his friends and they looked serious. '*Bhai dekh lo*. You have called me here, but you'll all face a boycott for associating with me. Today we are the pariahs of Karoran. I still don't know what our fault is,' Narinder began with some trepidation.

But Darshan gave him a friendly slap on the back and pushed him into an empty chair. 'Come here and sit next to me. We will all pay the fine for associating with you. We are with you, Narinder.' They told him that they did not approve of the social boycott announced by the khap panchayat against his family. 'If it is a question of the honour of the community and village then both Manoj and Babli are responsible for sullying it. The boycott should have been for both families,' said Sukhi.

They all began speaking together. At first Narinder could hardly register what was being said: he was so taken aback. He heard Darshan saying, 'Why has Babli's family been exempted? It's also unfair to put a boycott on the girls of your family. What is their crime? Is the honour of Karoran only linked to Babli? As the daughters of this village, the honour of Seema and Rekha is also important.'

'Does it behove the village community to force them to run to town for their daily needs in local buses?' said another man whom Narinder knew vaguely from his schooldays. As the voices swirled around him, a warm, comforting tingle began rising in his limbs. For the first time in days, he smiled. 'Thank God, some people have begun to dissent and assert themselves,' he thought to himself.

'Look, Narinder, you are from our Padra patti and, in solidarity, we have resolved that we will not break our association with your family,' they were saying.

Darshan pulled at Narinder's arm. 'Come on boys, let's all go to Manoj's house for a cup of tea.' They trooped out, with Narinder and Darshan leading the way.

After days of threats and loneliness, Chandrapati was delighted to receive them. Seema and Rekha emptied the last bit of powder from the milk packet and made tea for everybody. The men said that they would pool their money to collect the fine of 25,000 rupees to pay the khap, if it insisted.

Sure enough, the very next day, leaders of the khap took them to task for defying the boycott and threatened to impose a similar boycott on their families too. The parents of some of the men tried to placate the khap leaders by saying, 'You know how boys are nowadays. We have no control over them, but we'll talk them out of it. They won't defy the panchayat again. Let them be for now.' The boycott threat remained in the air but perhaps sensing that they would lose face if they insisted too much the khap leaders left. It was now up to the parents to talk their sons out of their defiance. Darshan and the others did not pay the fine, but there was no more show of solidarity from them in the coming days. The elders had clearly prevailed.

In Chandrapati's household, though, it was the one silver lining in the otherwise dark cloud over their lives, and the family slept a little easier that night.

Except that, unknown to them, the decomposed bodies of her son and daughter-in-law had been cremated at a municipal cremation ground in Rohtak that evening.

Chapter Four

'I Beg of You, Give Me Two Asthi Kalash'

The mystery of the missing newly-weds, Manoj and Babli, was hogging newspaper headlines in Haryana and Chandigarh. The recovery of Manoj's blue-and-white sports shoe from the Arjaheri toll plaza, the contractor Kuldeep Singh's statement and his description of the actual kidnapping were duly reported in newspapers, big and small, and questions began to be raised about why the police was not rounding up the kidnappers. The subsequent call for social boycott against Manoj's family had also got media coverage. Media persons, especially from language papers and television channels, were vying with each other to sniff out news about the couple. The Karnal district police and in particular the Butana police station came under the magnifying glass. Hacks on the crime beat began calling up Subhash Chand, SHO of Butana thana, every evening to get the day's update on the case, and when they got nothing new to report, they wrote that the police had made no progress. It kept up the pressure.

All this made Mandeep, the driver of the Scorpio in which Manoj and Babli had been kidnapped, increasingly nervous. In the first few days following his adventure on 15 June, he had bragged to his driver mates at the Kaithal civil hospital taxi stand that he had 'personal knowledge that the couple has been done away with'.

'How do you know?' They were curious.

'Arre, this Scorpio which is being mentioned in the newspapers is mine,' he had told them with a swagger. 'I had dropped them near Karoran and, from what I could see, things did not look good for them that day,' he had claimed, at his tea stall hang-out. But now that the registration number of his Scorpio had been published in one newspaper, prompting his employer, Rakesh Singh, to question him, he wasn't feeling so confident. Unknown to him, Narinder, disenchanted by the lackadaisical and even unhelpful attitude of the police in Kaithal, was conducting his own investigation into the kidnapping and Mandeep's loud talk at the taxi stand had reached his ears. He informed the Butana police about Mandeep's Scorpio. And, at around 6 p.m. on 26 June, when Mandeep was returning from a nearby village where he had gone to drop a patient's family, SHO Subhash Chand stopped him at Pehowa Chowk and arrested him. That was to be the end of Mandeep's carefree days.

The next day he was produced before a magistrate who remanded him to police custody for seven days. In the next two days he not only identified the spot from where Manoj and Babli had been kidnapped at the toll plaza but also the place in the fields near Karoran where he had dropped them along with their kidnappers. In his disclosure statement, he referred to Gangaraj as the person who had been sitting with him in the vehicle throughout the journey from Kaithal to the Arjaheri toll plaza, the one who was constantly on the phone, giving instructions to the others. Mandeep told the police that the Scorpio HR05M-4748 was parked in Jaipur, in his friend Karambir's house, as he was scared about the fallout of the incident. But the next day he changed his statement and took the police to his employer's house in Kaithal town, where the Scorpio had been parked all along. It was taken into custody.

30 June

Narinder had virtually taken charge as the head of their family and Chandrapati could only sigh with relief. 'Bless him. What would we have done without him?' she thought, as she packed lunch for him. Today he was going to the Butana police to find out if they had any news and also to his Karnal office, to get his leave extended. Seema had been in and out of home the last few days as she had to go to Jaipur frequently to appear for her exams. But today she was home and Chandrapati felt somewhat reassured—Seema's absence generally left her uneasy. These days, she was often overcome by an odd urge to keep her brood close to her, almost like a hen that huddles her chicks under her wings. It irritated Seema, who wanted to accompany Narinder whenever he went out to search for information about Manoj and Babli. But Chandrapati was reluctant to let her go except when it seemed absolutely necessary.

When Narinder reached Butana police station around mid morning, a head constable on duty told him about the VT message sent by Narnaund police station on 23 June about the recovery of the bodies of a boy and a girl. 'They could be that of Manoj and Babli! Has anyone verified their identity?' Narinder wanted to know. But the policemen had no more information to give him.

He was determined to find the bodies of Manoj and Babli and get to the bottom of this matter. But how?

He doubled back to his office and used a colleague's desk to draft a statement for the local press. By now he had begun to understand the power of the media and the importance of keeping them informed. It became his force multiplier. The *Dainik Bhaskar* and some other vernacular newspapers carried the news of the recovery of two bodies at Narnaund.

They asked if these bodies were Manoj's and Babli's and questioned why the Karnal police had not acted on the information, when they had a complaint of kidnapping before them. Stung, the police machinery finally began to respond.

1 July

The investigation of the Manoj and Babli abduction case had been handed over to the Criminal Investigation Agency (CIA) II of the Karnal police and Inspector Amar Dass was put in charge. By mid morning Jaspal Singh, sub-inspector at the CIA II, had reached Karoran and told Chandrapati and Seema that they would have to go with him to Narnaund to identify the clothes found on the two bodies. Narinder's gambit had worked.

The two women got into the police Gypsy along with Narinder and headed towards Narnaund. It was a muggy day and paddy planting was in full swing in the countryside. Chandrapati and Seema sat silently in the back seat, lost in their thoughts. Narinder too was as nervous as his aunt and cousin. At Narnaund police station, HC Rajesh Kumar showed them three bundles wrapped in cloth. Seema wrinkled up her nose, thrown by the stench from the bundles. A grim Chandrapati began opening one of the bundles, and they realized that the clothes were covered with live, inch-long maggots. Her voice breaking, Seema requested the SHO if he could get the clothes cleaned as it was difficult to identify them because of the dirt. Blandly, the man told them they could use the tap and soap outside. As they washed the clothes, Chandrapati recognized Manoj's pink shirt within minutes.

She broke down. The finality of the evidence before her eyes was unbearable. They also identified Babli's anklets, and six brass bangles and a brass ring they had gifted her in Chandigarh. She had been wearing them when she was killed. Her green kurta and black salwar too were easily identifiable. The third bundle contained the ropes used to tie their bodies and the sack in which Manoj had been wrapped.

Seema had begun to cry softly and Narinder held her in a brotherly hug. Her father had died when she was five years old and she did not remember crying for him because she had hardly known him. But Manoj and she had grown up together, quarrelled for their mother's affections, and shared a close bond. Even though all the signs had pointed to Manoj's being killed, she had been hoping against hope these last few days that he would somehow surface from wherever he was hiding, just like he had after eloping with Babli in April. 'How could I be so foolish? Do the dead ever come back?' she admonished herself.

It was late afternoon when they reached Butana. Now that the belongings of Manoj and Babli had been identified, Chandrapati's original FIR of abduction was converted to murder and sections 302, 201 and 120 B of the IPC were added to it. Narinder again called up his friends in the media and the Butana police station was soon swarming with reporters, pressing all kinds of questions on the policemen present there. By the end of the day, the police had arrested Suresh, Rajinder and Gurdev from Karoran.

Meanwhile, Chandrapati, Seema and Narinder were searching for a place to spend the night in Karnal. SHO Jaspal Singh, who had taken them in his Gypsy, refused to drop them back to their village. When Narinder requested him, he said he did not have permission. Beaten and heartbroken by the day's events, they headed towards a gurdwara hoping to get some food there. Sitting on fraying mats on the floor, they picked at the chapattis and dal served to them from the langar. It was late in the night when they finally found a dharamsala which had one room to offer. The fan in their room did not work but they hardly noticed the heat. Yet another man from their family had died. A gruesome death, the evidence of which had left them traumatized. Seema was overcome by remorse at not having been present at the Kaithal court on 15 June, the day they were abducted and murdered. She had just returned from Jaipur that morning and, since it was a Friday, she was fasting. 'Why, oh why, did I not go to Kaithal? Maybe I could have averted their murder. I could have helped . . .' she sobbed.

Chandrapati was scraped out hollow. When she had set off from Karoran that morning, Manoj's death was still in the realm of conjecture. Though fear and uncertainty were her constant companions, she lived in hope that Manoj was safe somewhere. But now she knew for sure that she had lost him. She remembered her last conversation with him. The tears, pent up for weeks, gushed out. The two women hugged each other as they wept late into the night.

*

The next day's papers splashed the story of the identification of Manoj's and Babli's clothes and how the two bodies recovered by the Narnaund police had been cremated as unclaimed at Rohtak. Some newspapers had carried a separate news item on the late-evening arrests of Suresh, Rajinder and Gurdev, which must have given the Karnal police a breather. Their boss, Arshinder Chawla, SSP at

Karnal, was personally monitoring the case and Inspector Amar Dass probably knew the sooner he caught the others the better it would be for him. A day later, on 2 July, he arrested Satish from Jakhauli village and all four were remanded to police custody till 4 July.

The four accused were still in a state of shock when they were put in the police lock-up in Karnal. The cell stank of urine and decay. They squatted on the floor and Suresh was the first to speak. 'How did this happen? Do you all remember how Gangaraj assured us that not a lock of our hair would be harmed? And now here we are, all in this stinking lock-up and he and Baru Ram are free.'

'I don't know about you all but I am certainly going to tell the police that they are as much involved in this as we are. Why should they get away?' Gurdev growled from the corner where he had made himself comfortable against the wall. The others nodded in agreement. They knew well that there was very little they could hide, when interrogated by these tough Karnal policemen. They were not like the policemen of Rajaund who had understood the shame Babli had brought upon the family and community. Just the thought of her made Suresh grit his teeth.

On 3 July Inspector Amar Dass took them to the toll plaza and the fields near Karoran and they were made to identify the spot from where they had kidnapped the two and the spot where they had been murdered. They made almost identical disclosure statements. Suresh and Gurdev told the police that they had laid Manoj on the ground and removed his pants and socks. All of them had joined in to beat him. Then Baru Ram, Gurdev and Suresh had held him while Rajinder strangulated him with the help of a rope. Satish admitted to removing Manoj's wristwatch. 'All five of us threw the dead body of Manoj along with the rope and that of Babli after tying her feet with the rope into the running water of the Sirsa Branch canal near Jind Road, Narwana, by carrying the bodies in the diggi (boot) of the car. When we were coming along, it came to my mind that I should not keep any item of the deceased with me and so I threw the watch. I do not remember where I threw it,' he told the policemen.

Rajinder told the police that he had taken Manoj's mobile phone from the pant pocket and had thrown the clothes and phone into the canal after Manoj's body. Gurdev said that he had removed Manoj's wallet with some money in it and a photograph of him and Babli. He had hidden the wallet under some bricks near Sajjan Singh's fields and took the police to that spot. While they were in that area, Baru Ram drove past in his car HR09-6500. Almost simultaneously Gurdev and Suresh pointed at him. 'He is Baru Ram and that is the car in which we put Manoj's and Babli's dead bodies while taking them to the canal.' Inspector Amar Dass could not believe his luck at netting yet another suspect. Baru Ram was the fifth person to be arrested.

Mandeep's Scorpio was meanwhile vacuumed and the police recovered a torn photograph of Manoj and Babli, a piece of Babli's anklet, a hair clip and shards of glass bangles. Baru Ram's Maruti car was similarly cleaned and a door handle with blood smeared on it was sent to the forensic laboratory for examination.

*

Jagmati Sangwan was in the middle of a late-evening meeting with activists of the Akhil Bhartiya Janwadi Mahila Samiti, a women's activist group she headed in Haryana. They were in the small room which served as their office in Rohtak's Jasbir Colony. For the last three days, ever since it had become known that Manoj and Babli had indeed been killed and it was their bodies that had been cremated as unclaimed at Rohtak, she and her band of activists in Kaithal and Hisar had been in touch with Manoj's family, consoling them and providing support to help them fight back. Her cell phone flashed. Her caller informed her that an interview of Seema and Chandrapati was being broadcast on a local news channel. They quickly tuned in and heard Seema describe how they had identified the belongings recovered from the dead bodies of Manoj and Babli. She talked of their sorrow at not being able to give the couple a proper funeral. Their bodies, considered as unclaimed, had been cremated in Rohtak, a mere 150 kilometres from Karoran. Turning towards her workers, Jagmati wondered, 'Is it possible to trace the cremation ground where the cremations were carried out? We really should do something to alleviate this family's misery.'

The next day she and a couple of others went to the office of the Rohtak municipal committee, where they were told that the Narnaund police had cremated two bodies on 24 June at the municipal cremation ground. 'The ashes might still be there, because a platform is cleared only when it is needed for cremating another body. In the case of unclaimed bodies we usually wait for a few days, as some relative might turn up to claim the ashes,' a municipal official told them.

They hurried to the cremation ground, found the platform untouched, and collected the ashes. Jagmati immediately called up Narinder to tell him that she had the ashes and would be bringing them to their village herself the next day.

In Karoran, the family began preparing for the funeral. Chandrapati went to the house of the village potter to buy an asthi kalash, the traditional pot of baked mud, to hold the ashes. It did not strike anyone in the house that the boycott would extend even to funeral preparations. The potter was unloading a fresh lot of clay from the buffalo cart in his courtyard when she walked in. He stopped her before she could reach his workplace. 'Go away. We are not allowed to talk to you,' he shouted.

'You know very well that my son has died. I beg of you to give me two asthi kalash to carry his ashes. I will always remember your favour,' said Chandrapati, as she wiped a tear with the corner of her dupatta. But the potter had turned his face.

'How many Diwali diyas and water pots I have bought from this potter in better times! Just look at him, now he turns me away,' she thought as she moved on unhappily.

Back home, Seema, hauling up her last reserves, called up a college friend who lived in Pai, a small town some seven kilometres away, to see if she could help get the pots. Her friend reassured her that she would arrange for them. Just as she put the phone down, Jagmati and T.K. Rajalakshmi, the *Frontline* correspondent who had been reporting the case, walked in. They had entered the village discreetly and no one had seen them bringing the ashes. But after spending some time with Chandrapati and her family, Jagmati told Rajalakshmi, 'I think we should also visit Babli's house to offer condolences. Her widowed mother needs to be comforted.'

The two made their way towards Billa patti at the other end of the village and just as they neared Babli's house Jagmati slowed her steps on seeing a group of men sitting outside. She covered her head and addressed them: 'Bhaiyo, we would like to meet Ompati.'

The one nearest to her looked her up and down and said, 'You cannot meet her.' She hesitated, wondering what to say next. The group stirred and a youngish man got up. 'You women are responsible for fuelling this fire. You have brought a bad name to our village. Ompati does not need your condolences. Go away.'

Two more men got up menacingly and warned the women that if they did not leave immediately they would wreck their car. They retreated without another word. Jagmati could see that arguing would be counterproductive. Reasoning and tolerance were in short supply that day and no one wanted to hear anything.

Seema caught the first bus for Pai at five the next morning, to buy the asthi kalash and other items required for the funeral ceremony. When she returned, the whole village knew that the family had managed to procure the pots and watched as she and Vinod walked to their house. Not a soul stepped out of their door to assist them or offer condolences.

Later, when the small funeral procession wound its way through the narrow lanes, Ompati came to the first-floor window as they passed her house and paid silent homage to her dead daughter. She had a veil over her face and no one saw her tears. Seema and Narinder were holding the pots tied with a red cotton cloth and they were followed by Mahavir and his wife, Vinod and two of Narinder's friends from the locality. The procession headed towards the kab, an ancient pond on the outskirts of Karoran, where the funeral ashes from several villages around have been immersed for centuries. The kab is said to be blessed with the divinity of five tiraths (pilgrimage places) held sacred by Hindus. Legends connect it to the Bhagvad Purana and villagers believe that in the hoary past it had steps of gold.

Their neighbours and acquaintances stood silently in their doorways and watched them walk past. Men, women and children from other localities gathered in the streets, but none dared to walk a step along with them. There was no chanting of mantras because the pundit had refused to conduct the rituals. It was a bizarre spectacle, unlike any funeral ceremony in living memory across Haryana.

At the kab, the small group of mourners stood on one side of the pond as they immersed the ashes. On the opposite side was gathered almost the whole village, silent and detached purveyors of the misery of this wretched, desolate family.

*

Ompati's clothes hang on her thin frame. She flings a dupatta randomly over her head when visitors come calling, and all that one can see of her face on these occasions is a prominent nose that stands out on a gaunt, acne-scarred face. Babli didn't look anything like her mother. Her big eyes, set in a round, fair face, and other features were all from her father. Her brother Suresh too has the same good looks. But mother and daughter shared a close bond, wrought perhaps out of common suffering during their frequent stand-offs against the men of the family, who ruled them with an iron hand. Many in the village say that Ompati is the only voice of reason in their household, and she usually manages to get the men to agree to her viewpoint with a clever combination of tact and logic. But Babli had seen her buckling down on many occasions, and wished her mother was more assertive.

People in Karoran insist that if Ompati had her way Manoj and Babli would not have died. She was the one who pleaded with her brother-in-law, brother and son to spare her daughter. Her reasoning: everyone would forget the girl's crime after some time. Why should they lose a child? But her voice was lost in the angry churn that simultaneously whipped up passions of family and community honour.

As the saga of police and media inquisitions played out in their village, Ompati's silence was puzzling. In the days following the murder, the men in her family never allowed her to talk independently, and if anyone insisted on speaking with her she was always accompanied by male members of the family. No one in the media got to ask her whether she approved of her daughter's killing by her own son and relatives. She grieved for her daughter as only a mother can. Alone in her sorrow within the four walls of her house where she was confined in the months that followed the deaths. Were they worried that she would crack up and reveal all? Was she the weak link in Babli's clan, who did not stand in solidarity with the others? Or was she a silent, helpless spectator? Did she weep for Babli? More pertinently, was she even allowed to?

Chapter Five

'The Law Will Take Its Course'

It used to take Seema a good ten hours by bus to reach Jaipur from Kaithal. In better times, she had enjoyed the early-morning routine of getting up before daybreak to catch the first bus going to Jaipur; she loved to keep the window open, feel the rush of the breeze sliding the dupatta off her head, and revel in a sense of purposefulness. She was the first in her family to venture so far from home to study. Jaipur was exciting, exotic.

She had enrolled at the Sanjay Law College for a three-year law degree and had taken a paying guest (PG) accommodation with two other girls. Together they watched Hindi movies on their days off, and the girls laughed at her fascination for movies which featured the police, lawyers or judges. She found the court scenes riveting. The law degree was her vehicle to a better life, away from the oppressive confines of Karoran, where girls like her were frowned upon. But, with the events of the last few weeks, the tentacles she was trying to escape seemed to close in on her. Each time she boarded a bus for Jaipur to appear for an exam, she worried about her mother and siblings back home. With so much happening at home, she knew she wouldn't get good marks. All she wanted now was to somehow scrape through the first year, but even that was appearing difficult. Ever since Manoj and Babli had disappeared from Pipli, she had not had a day's respite.

The police had arrested Suresh, Baru Ram, Satish, Gurdev, Rajinder Singh and Mandeep Singh, the driver of the Scorpio in which Manoj and Babli had been kidnapped. But instead of providing the family a breather, the arrests made things worse for them. Apart from their own Banwala khap and other self-styled leaders from Karoran, khaps from across Haryana launched a relentless crusade against her family. Seema was filled with trepidation as she thought of what lay ahead.

Enraged by the arrests, one or the other khap panchayat issued statements threatening 'dire consequences' if the accused were not released, and these began appearing in newspapers every other day. The rash of panchayat meetings was also aimed at sending a message to the political leaders in the state. It had the desired effect and alarm bells began ringing in the Haryana civil secretariat at Chandigarh and in Rohtak, the unofficial capital of Jatland and home to the state's Congress chief minister, Bhupinder Singh Hooda. There was not a word of condemnation from any mainstream political party about the brutal murders or a word of sympathy for the harassed family of Chandrapati. When pressed for a comment by the media, politicians resorted to the stock reply: 'The law will take its course.'

It was quite obvious to Chandrapati that no one from the village or elsewhere would raise their voice or come to their assistance, if they were attacked. She realized she would have to do something fast.

Bigger than the average Haryana village, Karoran is divided roughly into four pattis or localities and even before the Manoj–Babli affair blew up, there was a rift between Billa patti, where Babli's house is situated, and Padra patti of Manoj's house. It wasn't surprising, therefore, that most of those who came out in support of the killings and mobilized villagers for the boycott panchayat were from Billa patti. The rest of the village had fallen in line with the majority opinion. Fear of ostracism and intimidation forced the few dissenters to keep their opinions to themselves.

A few days after they had immersed the ashes, Chandrapati asked Seema to take Vinod and Rekha with her to Jaipur. 'I will stay here and face them. Attacking a poor old woman like me will shame them, but you must leave the village for some time,' she urged them. Rekha had dropped out of school a year ago, but Vinod was in Class X. It had become difficult for him to attend school. Chandrapati was apprehensive of the danger posed by the powerful men in Karoran—men like Gangaraj, the Congress leader who had evaded arrest, the village sarpanch Karambir and their cronies. Gangaraj had been named by Mandeep as a key conspirator of the kidnapping at the Arjaheri toll plaza, but it was openly and stridently being said in Karoran and many other villages, 'We will not allow the police to arrest him.' Manoj's family had become an eyesore for the villagers. They had not only brought shame and ignominy on Karoran, but had got upholders of their caste's honour arrested by the police.

Vinod and Rekha were loath to leave their mother alone. 'I will not run away from here like a coward. This is our home and we have nowhere else to go,' said Vinod in a voice which told Chandrapati that, even if he was the youngest in the house, he had grown up in the last few days. Rekha had a mulish look on her face as she squatted near the hearth, rolling chapattis for lunch. Furiously, she patted the dough with her palms and spread it out with the rolling pin, her shoulders rocking back and forth. The matter of their going away from the village did not come up again.

*

It was early July and there was no sign of the monsoon. A week's delay can be critical for the paddy crop. Millions of gallons of water, lying in deep aquifers, were pumped up using hundreds of diesel-guzzling gensets. Across Haryana and Punjab, the instinctive response of farmers to water shortage is to sink tube wells deeper and deeper, with no thought for the depleting water table and its catastrophic consequences. It is a hydrologist's nightmare but try telling that to the average farmer. Paddy farming brings them assured returns. Its support price is used as a handy political tool by governments to woo the farmers. In Haryana, the Jats, who are mainly farmers and comprise 22 per cent of the population, dominate, and woe betide the politician who does not pander to them. The powerful khaps around Karoran knew this only too well.

Now journalists began flocking to Chandrapati's modest house. They dropped in at odd hours for interviews, to hear about the latest twist in their case or the gossip about the social boycott. Even when the monsoon rains finally hit the village, pocking the parched mud paths with puddles of diluted cow urine and dung, these city slickers wrinkled their noses, picked their way past ponderous buffaloes and continued to knock on Chandrapati's door. She hated it, but Narinder patiently explained to the family one evening that they must never be rude to the media. 'Tell them the truth and share your problem with them. They are your protection against these people.' The family learned to face the cameras and talk coherently into mikes, though Rekha could never get over her shyness when the camera zoomed in on her. She would hide in the kitchen whenever anyone came with a video camera.

In the coming days, the JMS joined the media chorus demanding the arrest of the remaining conspirators and police protection for Manoj's family. None of this had escaped the attention of the khap leaders in the village and, along with Manoj's family, JMS activists too had become persona non grata in Karoran.

She will never know it, but Chandrapati actually earned the rock-solid support of the JMS. The organization was already fighting honour killings in Haryana, but its activists had some reservations about taking up the Manoj–Babli case. Jagmati had chaired a special meeting at their cramped, dusty office in Rohtak's Jasbir Colony to discuss the issue and convince the sceptical members. The words of Kamlesh, their representative from Fatehbad, had rung loud through the meeting: 'Dekho ji, this is an intra-gotra issue. We all know that marrying within the same gotra is not accepted in our society. How will we explain to the people our support for this family?'

She was backed by a few others. Sushila spoke next: 'This has to be carefully thought through. We have been opposing honour killings throughout the state but I think we should be cautious in extending help to the family of Manoj as this can have a deleterious impact on the JMS itself. Today, our campaigns are well received by the people. But if we are seen to be supporting an intra-gotra marriage, we risk the danger of being isolated in society.'

Jagmati heard them out. But all along her mind kept going back to the television interview of Chandrapati and Seema that she had seen. Their grief and determination to take the case to its logical conclusion had convinced her that this was a family who could fight this problem if they received sufficient support. She looked up and cleared her throat to speak. 'What you say is right. But as you all know, the JMS is against injustice. Our stand has always been that honour killings are murder and the law of the land should apply to them. Murder, however much justified by society, cannot be tolerated in any civilized society. If we restrict ourselves to just this much, we should be fine.' Shakuntala Jakhar and Sheela agreed with her and took it upon themselves to convince the resistant members. They were mostly new entrants to the JMS. By the time the meeting ended, they had chalked out a programme of how they would raise the pitch statewide as well as at the national level.

The JMS, better known in media circles of Delhi in its English avatar as the All India Democratic Women's Association (AIDWA), is affiliated to the Communist Party of India (Marxist), CPI(M), one of the country's two leading left political parties. In Haryana though, the party has a fringe presence and rarely manages to win an assembly seat. But as far as social reform is concerned, the JMS is highly vocal and visible, and is at the forefront of campaigns against the powers wielded by Jat khaps. Paradoxically, the zeal of its activists is seen as one reason for the party's inability to expand its hold in the conservative, hidebound, Jat-dominated state, so resistant to social change. To their credit, this hasn't in any way deterred its activists.

One of them is the slim and petite Shakuntala Jakhar in Hisar. Her short hair is usually covered with a cotton dupatta, a cotton bag hangs from her shoulder and on her feet are no-nonsense floaters. Her rich, deep voice is at total variance with her feminine frame and she has learned to use it on the phone to gain instant respect from sundry government officials.

As the general secretary of the JMS, Shakuntala had all but adopted Manoj's family in those days. She and Premchand, of the Democratic Youth Federation of India, another CPI(M) affiliate, were among the few people who regularly visited Chandrapati's house. Sometimes, they would find a padlock hanging on the door. But Seema had told Premchand that it was a ruse to make people think that they were not at home. A safety measure! He had taken to knocking quietly and calling for Seema or Chandrapati through a crack and on hearing his familiar voice they would open the door. He invariably wore a brown khadi kurta and sunglasses, and had matching hennaed hair. Whenever he came to Karoran, it was on a borrowed motorbike and he took care to keep out of sight of Billa patti. Premchand kept a protective eye on the family.

One rain-soaked afternoon, when Chandrapati was telling a journalist from Kaithal about the hardship they had to face because of the boycott, Jagmati called from Rohtak. She advised Chandrapati to approach the National Commission for Women (NCW) in Delhi for help. 'We will accompany you to Delhi and assist you in submitting a formal complaint before the commission,' she said kindly. By now Chandrapati had come to trust the JMS. Shakuntala Jakhar and Sheela from Hisar had been in constant touch with her and Seema, advising and supporting them, at some risk to themselves. However, each new brush with the law or a government functionary left Chandrapati confused. She had never heard of the NCW. She hesitated for a moment before gathering her thoughts, and then said, 'You know what is best for us, behenji. I am an illiterate village woman who does not understand this paperwork. But if you think it can help us, then Seema and I will come with you.'

The rains had disappeared again and the countryside steamed under the hot sun when Shakuntala took a bus for Rohtak. She had asked Premchand in Kaithal to accompany Chandrapati, Seema and Narinder to Rohtak and there Jagmati joined them. They were on their way to the NCW. On the way to Delhi, Jagmati told them that the AIDWA president Brinda Karat (a Lok Sabha MP) had arranged for them to go to the National Human Rights Commission (NHRC) and that they would be submitting a complaint there too. Seema struggled to comprehend all this as she took in the sights and sounds of Delhi. Narinder kept a pen ready in his shirt pocket and took but a moment to whip it out whenever the trio had to sign anything. By the end of the day the NCW had issued directions to the Kaithal police to provide Chandrapati's family security and accepted their request to send a fact-finding team to Karoran to see things for themselves. The NHRC did not respond.

Seema and Chandrapati entered Karoran the next day with two policemen accompanying them. People watched askance. 'How did these two seemingly helpless women manage it?' they wondered. The cops, armed with pistols, positioned themselves near the main entrance of the house and anyone knocking on Manoj's house now had to first get past them. When they went off duty at the end of the day, they were replaced by two others for the night shift. By the end of the day word had spread like wildfire that the NCW team would be visiting Karoran. Gangaraj and his cronies began preparations to step up the pressure. Jat organizations across the state had to be mobilized.

*

The All India Adarsh Jat Mahasabha kicked off a massive campaign across the state to put pressure on the NCW 'to remain within its limits' when it came to Karoran. Its president, Dr Pavanjit Banwala, who also happened to be the then head of the Banwala khap, had spent the last few days in active consultation with Jat leaders. 'These left organizations have begun crossing all limits. It is shameful how most of their workers, themselves from the Jat community, are bent on destroying our age-old traditions,' he had fumed at a small gathering in his village the previous evening. Some people present were reportedly livid that Chandrapati had called Babli her daughter-in-law. 'How could she refer to a girl from this village like that? Had she lost her head?' they raged.

Another man felt they should collect at Kaithal in huge numbers to demonstrate their strength. The next day, all kinds of cars, bullock carts, buffalo carts, motorcycles, Tata Sumos and what have you offloaded hundreds of members of the Jat Mahasabha at the Jat Bhawan in Kaithal. Dr Pavanjit Banwala was the star speaker, who drew maximum applause with his incisive attack.

He denounced the Manoj and Babli affair and marriage as a blot on their religion and culture. He warned that the statements being issued by so-called social organizations in support of the guilty family and against the boycott, as a Talibanic diktat, would not be tolerated. The NCW team would be educated about the role of panchayats in preserving the social and cultural traditions of the Jats. The meeting was widely reported in the newspapers.

Hundreds of men from a host of other khaps across the state, such as the Nain, Mor, Punia and Beniwal khaps, had gathered. The air was thick with a rustic smell of sweat and smoke from bidis. But people on the stage caught a whiff of expensive perfume now and then. Among the speakers was the fetching and urbane Kusum Chaudhary, who was then the president of the women's wing of the Jat Mahasabha. As an aspiring politician, Kusum, who later joined the Congress, was a passionate advocate of khap supremacy in Haryana and took to the stage with élan. In that sea of grizzly, unshaved, unwashed men in kurta pyjamas, she stood out in her elegant salwar kameez and chiffon dupatta. She was the showpiece speaker, meant to convey the message that the Jat Mahasabha was not a 'men only' body but that women too supported its rules. It was unanimously decided that Kusum would be part of the Jat Mahasabha delegation which would meet the NCW team and apprise them of the Jat community's point of view.

Another organization, the All India Jat Brigade, joined the fray. At a similar though smaller meet, organized at its office in Kaithal, its president, Brajender Bangar, announced that they would oppose the NCW visit. Bangar called for an amendment 'in those laws which are ripping apart the fabric of our society'. The Kaur Jat Brigade also produced a woman leader of their own, Pushpinder Kaur, to support their stand. 'We sympathize with the family of Manoj, but will help them only if they abide by the norms of our Jat culture.' She rounded off her speech by warning the NCW to confine itself to the law and order problem and not to interfere in the internal matters of the Jat community. The Nain khap, the Dhul khap and many others held a series of meetings in the following days to keep up the pressure in the run-up to the NCW visit. Many said they would not allow the NCW team to visit Karoran.

From his modest office in the walled area of Kaithal, Premchand and his band of youth activists were keeping an uneasy watch on these developments. On 20 July, he submitted memorandums to the chief minister, the director general of police and the deputy commissioner of Kaithal, drawing their attention to the 'wanton statements, being made by caste panchayats to intimidate a constitutional body like the NCW'. Demanding action against the caste panchayats and their leaders who were making such statements, he also sought police protection for Chandrapati's family because they were being threatened and forced to withdraw their FIR. The stage was being set for the NCW visit and people wondered what would happen next.

*

It had rained the previous night and Seema got up to a muggy morning. As the day progressed, the heat became stifling, but that was the least of her worries. She slipped into a black and green printed salwar kameez and pulled out a black dupatta to go with it. She and Chandrapati, along with Narinder, were to go to Pundri, the sub-tehsil town fifteen kilometres away, to meet the NCW team at the rest house there. Chandrapati had worn her new blue printed salwar kameez and was throwing a bright red dupatta over her head when Seema intervened. 'Ma, at least today you should wear a matching dupatta with this suit. There will be so many people at the rest house. Rekha has a blue dupatta which you can borrow.'

'I am just fine. These "fashions" are for young girls like you,' said Chandrapati, and pulled the red dupatta once more over her head in her trademark no-fuss style, with its length falling back, like a nun's veil. It wasn't draped around the shoulders and bosom, like married women normally did. Her neck remained bare. It was how she wore the dupatta when she worked in the fields, or while patting cow dung cakes. Narinder in his new green shirt and cream pants smiled at the two women. He put all their documents and petitions in a polythene bag, stuck a pen in his shirt pocket and hurriedly downed the rotis and tea Rekha had made for them. Chandrapati wished there was some home-made butter to go with the rotis but the buffalo was still a couple of months away from delivering.

The Public Works Department rest house at Pundri was swarming with policemen, journalists, khap leaders and government officials. It is a squat colonial structure, with wide-arched verandas and high-ceilinged rooms. The smell of grimy carpets and decades of dampness clings to its walls at all times and patches of the old stone flooring can still be seen in some of its unused, abandoned rooms.

Pavanjit Banwala and Kusum Chaudhary along with other members of the Jat Mahasabha waited in the lawns to present their side of the story. So did Om Prakash Dhankar of the All India Jat Swabhiman Sabha, and his clutch.

Jagmati and her JMS activists waited in the veranda to submit a memorandum to the NCW team. They had changed their mind from the previous evening, when they had decided not to accompany the NCW team to Karoran, fearing their presence would vitiate the already tense atmosphere in the village. Seema and Narinder sat in the anteroom and began jotting down the sequence of events of the last few days on a piece of paper, to present to the team, when there was a commotion outside. Two senior members of the NCW, Yasmin Abrar and Malini Bhattacharya, who wanted to assess the problem for themselves, had arrived.

After briefly meeting the district officials, the two ladies indicated that they would like to meet Seema and Chandrapati alone. The officials waited outside and Seema told the two ladies about the boycott and threats they were getting from the village leaders to force them to withdraw their FIR. She also detailed the hardships they were facing in their day-to-day life in the village because of the boycott and the sustained harassment they had been subjected to by the Rajaund police. Yasmin and Malini heard them out calmly, though no doubt disturbed.

When it came to Jagmati's turn, news cameras zoomed in on her. Not mincing her words, she first attacked the police machinery. 'In the brutal killing of Manoj and Babli the dubious role played by the police administration should be inquired into and the guilty made accountable for their actions. Though there was proper proof that Babli was an adult and her marriage had been recognized by the Punjab and Haryana High Court, the Rajaund police showed her as a seventeen-year-old minor and registered a false case of kidnapping against Manoj and his mother and sisters,' she said in her trademark chaste Hindi. Coming from the Sangwan gotra, Jagmati belonged to the same Jat community whose actions she was deploring that day, and the Jat organizations hated her for that.

But Jagmati was determined to speak her mind that day. Looking into the cameras, she continued, 'At the same time, Manoj's mother's complaint about the kidnapping of her son was not registered, despite several visits to the police station. Again, when the sessions judge of Kaithal had ordered the police to provide protection to Manoj and Babli and reach them safely to their destination, the police left them unprotected midway, knowing full well that they were being followed by Babli's relatives. The police has, in a way, handed them over to their murderers.' She paused, to allow the journalists to absorb her point.

'Later, when the bodies of the couple were recovered from the Balsamand canal, the Narnaund police cremated them in such haste without even trying to verify who they were. This, despite there being a VT message from Butana police station about a kidnapped couple,' she said.

Jagmati also drew the attention of the NCW team and the media to the statements by Jat khaps, in the print and electronic media, that they would honour the people who had killed Manoj and Babli for upholding the values and ridding Jat society of an evil. 'At a time when the men accused of these murders are in jail, these organizations are openly cocking a snook at the law of the land. They are also issuing threatening statements against a constitutional body like the National Women's Commission. Why are the state government and police machinery not doing anything to check them?' she insisted. Shakuntala Jakhar and Premchand sat on either side of her.

At another end of the rest house, journalists had cornered Pavanjit Banwala and Kusum Chaudhary sitting under the shade of a tree with the banner of the Adarsh Jat Mahasabha fluttering behind them. The mustachioed Banwala wore a red badge with the mahasabha's insignia of two crossed swords and the slogan 'Jat Mahaan' on his sparkling white kurta. What he said that day sent shock waves among journalists present there and all those demanding implementation of the rule of law. 'Wherever in the country Jat couples marry into the same gotra, we will take harsh steps against them. Let there be no doubt about this.' A journalist wanted to know if the harsh steps included murder. 'If our society is polluted in this way, if brothers and sisters begin marrying each other, begin masturbating together, the whole social order will collapse. Murder becomes inconsequential in such a situation,' he replied.

'The Hindu Marriage Act, which recognizes such "sagotra" marriages as Manoj and Babli's as legal, goes against our culture and traditions. Either the government should amend the act and declare them illegal and punishable by law or we will boycott the law itself,' he announced in his well-known lisp. (The television cameras recorded every bit of his statement and Pavanjit's stand was widely aired on the channels.)

Kusum adjusted the sunglasses on her head and lectured the journalists about the festival of Raksha Bandhan and how same-gotra weddings were polluting the sanctity of the brother-and-sister relationship. The reporters who had missed out on Banwala's sound bite scrambled to get copies of it from their more lucky colleagues. There was a small kerfuffle in their ranks and the scene then shifted to Karoran.

The heat had become oppressive by the time Yasmin and Malini, accompanied by Rajinder Kataria, deputy commissioner of Kaithal, and Rajender Singh, SSP, reached

Chandrapati's house. They sat on the string cots Rekha had set out for them in the veranda, and Chandrapati and Narinder immediately began fanning the visitors with small hand fans. It helped to keep the flies away, but only just. Fanned away from the visitors, they parked themselves on the walls of the veranda and courtyard and became observers.

'We are here to send a message to the village that they must not harass you any more. We will be talking to the sarpanch also, and if you have any problem in the future do not hesitate to inform DC sahib here,' said Yasmin, pointing to Rajinder Kataria.

'Madam, some of my friends who wanted to end the boycott were also threatened by the sarpanch and his associates. I've called some of them today to meet you,' said Narinder, nervously working the hand fan.

'He won't do it any more. We will talk to him. Doesn't he need votes for the next election?' Yasmin responded promptly.

Narinder once more pressed his point about the failure of the police to arrest Gangaraj. 'He is the biggest threat to us today and he roams free,' he said.

'Madam, you must talk to Babli's mother when you go to her house,' said Seema from the edge of the charpoy. 'It was a one-sided panchayat which announced the social boycott against us. Is this how panchayats are conducted?' The only time Chandrapati spoke was to second Seema's request that they meet Ompati. She seemed overwhelmed by the presence of officials in her small house and maintained a grim expression throughout, never once smiling.

The two women from the NCW tried to reassure the family. The posse of officials from the district administration and the police filled their small courtyard, but the NCW team did not fail to notice that no one from the village came to be with the stricken family.

In stark contrast, when they went to Babli's house in Billa patti, all those who mattered in the village, including the sarpanch and Pavanjit Banwala, were there to meet them. Ompati sat close to Sarpanch Karambir, with her head covered, but did not utter a word. Outside, a teeming throng had gathered to express solidarity with Babli's family. The official government vehicles, the overwhelming police security for the NCW team, which had been the target of hostile comments in the days leading up to this visit, the presence of the DC and SSP in their village, all created an unbearable excitement for the inhabitants. They lingered on the streets long after the officials left the village.

A few days later the NCW submitted its report to the government. It observed:

> There can be no doubt this is a most heinous and barbaric crime. It is all the more shocking when such violence is perpetrated in the name of culture. Everyone is free to follow the cultural practices of the community in our country, but the name of culture cannot be used to justify oppression and torture, leading to the bloody wastage of two young lives. While the question of 'gotra' is mainly operative here, one should also note the difference in the financial status of the two families. Would the murders have happened if Manoj came from an equally or more influential family? The boycott that seems to be continuing is evidence of the power of money . . .
>
> . . . In spite of there being ample opportunity in this case of saving two precious lives and later of identifying the bodies, the police have failed to do so. Whether money and influence played a role here has to be probed . . .

> . . . It does not seem to us that the pressure on Manoj's family to withdraw the cases would diminish on its own unless the administration takes a very strong stand.

It recommended:

1. Full protection for Manoj's family and administration to be vigilant against intimidation.
2. Enquiry has to be instituted to see whether the police were negligent in the execution of their duty and any person under suspicion of collusion should be removed from the case.
3. It should be properly enquired whether some people allegedly involved in the case and named by the driver are still outside police custody and if this is so, they should be immediately arrested.
4. Some economic rehabilitation of Manoj's family should be arranged by the administration since they are in great distress and danger. The younger brother and sisters should be allowed to continue their education.

The first casualty of the visit was the SSP of Kaithal, Rajender Singh, who was transferred within two months of his being posted there.

The Jat organizations were incensed at the NCW visit. They saw it as a loss of face and an attack on their self-respect. But it had a salutary effect in Karoran and the social boycott of Manoj's family began to lessen in the days that followed. The first to soften was the grocer Sudarshan. As Seema passed by his shop one day, he sent a boy after her with a message that she could buy groceries from him if she wanted. Next were the autorickshaw drivers who stopped objecting when the family approached them to go to Kaithal. Seema, though, always wondered how much of this was simply because losing a customer for so long was not good business.

The family ended the day by offering tea and biscuits to the two policemen guarding them. Happiness, however small, is meant to be shared.

*

'The state in Haryana today is such that criminals, rapists and murderers have all the right to live confidently and with pride, whereas young boys and girls have no right to love and have romantic relationships,' said Shubha, vice president of the Haryana JMS, speaking at a state-level convention organized by the JMS and the DYFI in Kaithal against the khap diktats. Seema and Narinder had been invited as special guests to tell their story before the assembly. It was predominantly a women's gathering, and many were from Jat families.

The two occupied corner seats and watched the proceedings with interest. Neither of them had ever been to a forum like this and Narinder mentally went over what he wanted to say. Among the activists present was Dr Ranbir Singh Dahiya, who said, 'The people who comprise these so-called khap panchayats that talk of preserving culture and traditions are themselves indulging in female feticide and exploitation of women. Since when has this become our culture and tradition?'

When Dr D.R. Chaudhary, former chairman of the Haryana Public Service Commission, was introduced, Seema sat up with interest. She had heard of him from Shakuntala and watched the grey-haired academic walk on to the stage. She clapped the hardest when he said, 'Khap panchayats generally terrorize and harass the poor and helpless. But when well-off and influential families break social norms, khaps look the other way.'

'He is so right. But who listens to voices like his. Do you think the government will notice this convention?' she looked at Narinder and whispered.

The convention was aimed at sending a message that there was an equally vibrant and strong people's movement which would resist their atrocities.

Unlike Narinder, Seema needed no preparation to relate her story before the audience. After the initial few moments of stage fright, when she mumbled incoherently into the mike, she quickly warmed to her account. There were many moist eyes in the crowd when she walked off the stage, head shyly bowed and covered.

The two returned to Karoran, their spirits much bolstered. It felt good to see so many people on their side.

When they reached home, they found someone waiting for them. They could hardly recognize him in the fading evening light, but when Narinder came nearer he saw that it was Ranbir, a no-gooder from their own Padra locality. He was sitting cross-legged on a string cot in the courtyard and for a moment Narinder was puzzled. As far as he could remember, Ranbir was in jail for some offence. There were two more boys with him, whom he recognized as being from their patti.

'*Yoon na dekh bhai, mein parole le kar aaya hoon*'—Don't glare at me like that, I have come out on parole—Ranbir sought to answer their unspoken query. An uneasiness filled the house and Seema wondered what he could possibly want. They did not have to wait too long.

'While I was in Ambala jail, I met Suresh, Baru and others who are accused in the case filed by you all. They are full of remorse and regret and have asked me to convey to you that they would like a compromise. It is the only sensible thing to do—they are big and powerful and it's not in your interest to take up a lifelong enmity with them,' he began.

Seema stood still in the courtyard. Rekha too came out of the kitchen and stood in the doorway to listen.

Lowering his voice, Ranbir continued, 'They will pay you whatever you want. Just name a figure and you will get it. In return for taking back your FIR.' They looked on in shock. The thought of compromising with the killers of Manoj had never crossed their minds. So busy were they just coping with what life was flinging at them each day that the struggle seemed to have seeped into their selves.

'Compromise? An easy release from this struggle? But how would they be able to live happily, with the trade-off on their conscience? And what about the agony and pain that Manoj went through at their hands? Can I forget that? Should I?' thought Seema. Chandrapati was the first to break the spell.

She seemed to have made up her mind. 'Na bhai, Ranbir. This is not possible. We have lost our boy and daughter-in-law for no fault of theirs. And now their family is harassing us so much. We want justice. I will not give in to their alluring offer. No.'

'It will be better if you leave us to our fate. We can manage without Suresh's help,' said Seema taking up the cue.

Ranbir wasn't giving up easily. 'I would do a rethink if I were in your place. Don't be too confident of this police protection that you have . . .'

'Enough,' shouted Chandrapati. 'Ranbir, you better leave! Now! Don't force us to be nasty with you.'

It was the beginning of a sustained effort unleashed by the accused and their supporters to buy or force a settlement with Chandrapati so that she would withdraw her FIR.

*

Chandrapati is one of four daughters born to a middling farmer of Danauda, in Jind district. Not having a son rankled so deep with the old man that, when it came to dividing his property, he chose not to give it to any of his daughters but willed all his twenty-four acres of land to the eldest son of his eldest daughter. There was nothing extraordinary about his decision, because in their rural, patriarchal society it was quite unthinkable to hand over property to a woman. His contemporaries approved of his decision and neither Chandrapati nor her sisters ever contested it. That they had a right over their father's ancestral property was in the realm of government files and newspaper columns, not in the homes of rural Jat families like theirs who never questioned decisions on property taken by males. When Chandrapati was widowed at a fairly young age, she wished her father had not done this. Here she was living in penury, making ends meet by rearing buffaloes and single-handedly bringing up four children, when what was rightfully her share in the property was not hers to use. It hurt long and deep, especially because she used to be her father's favourite daughter while growing up.

Till the time her father-in-law, Hari Singh, was alive, she remained the submissive daughter-in-law, and he went out of his way to ensure that she and her children were well provided for. For the last decade or so, however, it was Chandrapati who headed her family as its men had died one after the other. She learned to go to Kaithal for sundry tasks connected with her children's education and contracted the two and a half acres of her husband's inheritance each year to whoever offered her the maximum money. She bought fodder and seed, sold milk and did all the things that were generally done by a man in their village. And this included dealing with the frequent quarrels that erupted around their neighbourhood. She guarded her turf and her children with a fierceness that only a mother, left on her own, can display. This was perhaps when she developed her own no-nonsense style of wearing a dupatta. Sometimes when Rekha oiled and plaited her hair, she arranged it gracefully over Chandrapati's head and shoulders, only to find it back in its usual place by the end of the hour. 'Ma, what is this?' Rekha would say, weakly reprimanding her mother, knowing well that Chandrapati did what suited her.

Narinder was not just the son of her husband's younger brother but her own sister's son. He was as much a loser as Chandrapati's children in his grandfather's inheritance and the two often talked of the injustice done to them by the old man. 'Taayi, one day we will challenge this matter in the court and get back our rightful share,' he would say during these discussions. But Chandrapati, already burdened with the weight of bringing up four fatherless children, would defer the matter. 'Yes we will, when we have some money to fight a court case. Let my Manoj stand on his feet and earn something, then we will see.'

Coping with life without a man in the house had brought out her innate toughness. She soon realized that there was hardly anything she could not do on her own. She had successfully thwarted attempts by distant relatives to usurp her small landholding, and that was when she began questioning silently the strict norms of male domination by which they lived. She resolved that her daughters should never have to submit to them. She became outspoken and aggressive and people in the Padra locality hesitated to cross swords with her. So even before Manoj and Babli were killed, Chandrapati had earned a reputation for being a poor but no-nonsense woman, who rarely hesitated to speak her mind. Some even call her a fighter.

Not surprisingly, the menfolk of Karoran hated her guts. They hated her for her independent ways and loved to spread salacious stories about her. She responded with a thickened hide and, in recent years, had even begun to enjoy bouncing off the darts aimed at her. Many of her husband's relatives in the village sided with the khap which boycotted them and openly denounced her as an 'unpleasant person' before the media which covered the meeting. It strengthened her inner resolve to fight back.

*

Gangaraj got up with a start. Ever since that wretched Chandrapati had filed an FIR against him, he hadn't got a good night's sleep. But today was not a day to worry about her, he thought as he went through his early-morning ablutions. There was an important meeting of Congress workers in Pundri and his friend and mentor Tejinder Singh Mann, the local legislator, was going to preside. The agenda was to discuss Chief Minister Bhupinder Singh Hooda's forthcoming visit to Karoran and Pundri on 27 September. As a senior Congresswala of the village, Gangaraj had much to do not only for today's meeting but to ensure that the chief minister's visit also went off well. He just hoped there wouldn't be any of those pesky press reporters at the meet. He hadn't invited any, but they seemed to hang around the local legislator and he was certain that at least the Kaithal-based reporters would have an eye on today's meeting.

With his role in the Manoj–Babli affair under the scanner, Gangaraj had begun to avoid the very journalists he had once patronized. They seemed to be everywhere and gleefully reported his presence in one or the other village, always raising the question: 'Why is the police saying that they cannot find him?' Mentally fuming at their 'disloyalty', he made his way towards the village chaupal, where there was already a large group of men. He noticed with satisfaction the presence of men from other localities. It made him feel good. He and the sarpanch Karambir got into one car and the others squeezed into a couple of other Maruti cars and left for Pundri in a cloud of dust.

Whenever Gangaraj appeared in public nowadays, he found people looking at him with awe. Already some Jat organizations had been in touch to invite him to their functions where they wanted to honour him. People in Karoran had begun to say, 'He is fast becoming a leader of the Jats. If things go this way, he might even get a ticket for the next assembly elections.' Mann addressed the gathering and informed them that the chief minister would be inaugurating a 33 KVA electricity substation and a primary health centre in Karoran. The village would also be made a model village under a special scheme. There was a brief discussion on some of the other problems the villages were to raise before the chief minister, but no one talked about the Manoj–Babli affair or the social boycott in force against Manoj's family. It was the 1st of September.

*

Sub-Inspector Jaipal Singh, at the Karnal crime branch, flung a copy of the *Dainik Bhaskar* on his table. 'Look at this, CM sahib is going to Karoran and Gangaraj is making preparations for the visit! Who will believe us when we say that we cannot find him? This is so embarrassing.'

Sitting across the room, Head Constable Ram Chander nodded his head. 'It's almost three months since the registration of the FIR and we will have to file the charge sheet in the court any day now.'

'These presswalas are raising hell. If one were to believe everything they write, then it seems as if we have done nothing in the case. You tell me, was it Manoj's ghost that went out and arrested the six others? And who got Gangaraj's phone records and did all the other running around to put the case together? Bastards! They have been hovering like vultures around our police station for the last three months. If I had my way I would strangle each one of them . . .' Jaipal said, wringing a neck in the air.

'You said it, SHO sahib,' said Ram Chander, and the police station erupted in laughter.

As soon as SHO Jaipal got into his vehicle and drove off, the others gathered for their daily gossip session, near the munshi's desk. 'I hear the SSP has asked us to be careful. There could be violence,' said a mustachioed constable who had recently been transferred from Kurukshetra.

Jasmer, sitting near the window, joined in. 'Of course. I for one wouldn't want to be in the arrest party. You never know with these chaps . . . No thank you!'

'It's tough to be a policeman nowadays. You'll get it both ways,' said another.

'Hmmm.' Jasmer spat out of the window, and watched his groggly land on the leaves of a limp periwinkle. 'The netas will skin us alive and make us forget the IPC too. Bhai, tell someone to get tea, I haven't had a cup since morning.'

On 21 September 2007, the Butana police filed a detailed charge sheet against the six accused persons in custody and told the court that despite sending him notices to join the investigation, and after raiding several places, Gangaraj, one of the main accused, could not be arrested. The charge sheet noted that in August the police had managed to get telephone records of calls made from Gangaraj's telephone number 9416563752 between 10 and 20 June 2007, which showed that he was present at the spots where the kidnapping and murders took place and that he was in constant touch with the other accused on the day of the murders. Soon after that, Head Constable Jai Inder of Rajaund police station was asked to join the investigation as the accused were found to have been in touch with him too, on the phone.

In Karoran, the mood in Gangaraj's camp was somewhat downbeat. Although he had managed to evade arrest, thanks to his contacts, he had been named in the charge sheet. It was not a good sign.

When Narinder told Seema that the charge sheet had been filed without arresting Gangaraj, she exclaimed, 'I knew it. They don't have the guts to arrest him. He is sitting here in his home and they can't touch him. Shameful!'

As if on cue, two more Jat panchayats immediately issued statements that they would oppose any move to arrest Gangaraj. They need not have bothered.

Six days after the Karnal police filed the charge sheet, the chief minister graced Karoran with a visit. Ironically, among those who welcomed him that day was Gangaraj. The deputy commissioner, the SSP of Kaithal and scores of policemen were among the swarm of officials accompanying the chief minister. No one gave Gangaraj, whose imposing figure always stands out in a crowd of supporters, a second glance. Neither did the chief minister bother to visit the humble house of Chandrapati and condole with her.

Two days later Tejinder Singh Mann addressed another workers' meeting at Kaithal to thank them for making the chief minister's visit a grand success. Gangaraj's presence was again duly reported in the newspapers the next day.

In Kaithal, Premchand pored over newspapers, and carefully collected as many clippings as possible as proof of the Karnal police's reluctance to arrest Gangaraj. 'Such a tragedy has befallen Manoj's family and the chief minister did not think it necessary to even visit them,' he mused.

His friend Shankar smiled. 'Of course he could not. What if Chandrapati had asked him to get Gangaraj arrested? Told him about their ostracism and begged for help? Would he help? No.'

Premchand rubbed a weary hand over his forehead. 'I suspect that his visit to the village is aimed at sending a message to the khaps that he is with them. Why else should he have gone to Karoran when the controversy there is still raging?'

*

Narinder was busy making pay cheques for the staff and had put his mobile phone on silent mode as he was in a hurry to finish the task before evening. But it lay on his desk and he saw an unknown number flashing on the device. Twice he ignored it but the flashing screen had begun to distract him and he eventually pressed the talk button to get the call out of the way. '*Narinder bhai bol rahe ho kya? Main Mann sahib ke office se bol raha hoon,*' said a voice at the other end.

From the deference in the voice on the line, Narinder guessed that he was referring to the legislator Tejinder Singh Mann. He was curious. What could the exalted Mann possibly want from him? 'Does he want to threaten me?' he wondered anxiously.

'*Haan bhai. Narinder bol reha hoon,*' he muttered into the phone and immediately walked out of the office with the device in his ears. He did not want half the office listening in on a conversation with the legislator's office.

'*Aisa hai,* Gangaraj and some people from Karoran want to meet you, to discuss Chandrapati's case. Mann sahib has personally requested that you should meet them. They want you to help them. Don't say no,' said the politico's man.

For a moment Narinder was stumped. But he recovered his wits and thought, there really is no harm in meeting them. He injected some steel into his voice and told the legislator's flunkey that he would meet them. 'Tell them to come to the Ror dharamsala near Karnal bus stand tomorrow,' he said, and called off. He then made a call to Arshinder Chawla, SSP, Karnal, and apprised him of the proposed meeting. 'Since I am alone, I will be grateful if you could depute some policemen for my security when they come to meet me,' Narinder requested. He had already been provided an armed guard following threats to his life and the SSP sent another two armed constables to the Ror dharamsala the next day.

Gangaraj and around twenty-five of his supporters from Karoran got on to a mini truck and reached the dharamsala at the appointed time. A nervous Narinder, who had grown scrawnier because of the events of the last few months, met them in a room, surrounded by his three security guards. It was a short conversation and later Narinder wondered if it would have gone differently had Chandrapati or Seema been there. Gangaraj did not say much; the others did the talking for him.

'Dekh Narinder,' said Om Prakash, 'we want this enmity between the two families to end. The police case has ruined the reputation of Gangaraj and Babli's family. We have just one request to make. You name a figure. We can pay up to one crore. Take it and persuade Chandrapati to withdraw the FIR.'

He had anticipated something like this but even so the figure quoted by them stunned him. It was way beyond anything he could have earned in his entire life as a clerk in the Haryana government. He wiped the sweat off his forehead and collected his thoughts, hid his trembling hands deep inside his trouser pockets and rocked on his heels to gain some confidence. He knew what his answer would be, and took a moment to find the right words for it.

When he finally replied, it was in a tone he had never heard himself use before: 'If I gave you two crores, would you let me kill two of your family members?'

Very little was said after that and the meeting wound up in a few moments.

CHAPTER SIX

'Just Name a Figure, Sir'

Lal Bahadur Khobal pushed back his chair and stretched. It had been a long day in the courts and he was in a hurry to get back home. His wife, Trishna, had called to say that she wanted him to take her shopping for decorations for their son's birthday. Traffic at the best of times in Hisar is a pain, and during the evening rush hour it is sheer madness. It would take him a good forty-five minutes of driving through endless jams, avoiding lunatic cyclists and stray cows, to reach home, and the thought of heading off to the market again wasn't alluring. His cell phone rang. It was Surat, his junior, who had been pestering him to meet a prospective client from his village. He changed his mind about going to the market and called Trishna to tell her to take a rickshaw and go on her own. 'I'll be late today. I've ordered the cake, so you needn't go to the bakery. Just pick up some balloons and bunting from a nearby shop,' he told her.

After Rohtak, Hisar is Haryana's most important town. Khobal's favourite drawing-room topic was how the bigwig politicians who lived here had done little for the uplift of this mofussil town. Its most famous resident was Bhajan Lal, Congress leader and long-time chief minister of Haryana. He was then in semi-retirement, having taken ill a few years ago after his political fortunes plummeted. The town is also home to the powerful Jindals who run the Jindal Steel empire, now spread over many states. The family patriarch O.P. Jindal had represented Hisar assembly constituency in the Haryana Vidhan Sabha and after his death his wife, Savitri, had taken over. Their son Naveen Jindal is a passionate aviator and the Lok Sabha MP from nearby Kurukshetra. People of Hisar know him mostly for his frequent rounds over the town in his personal helicopter. 'Why should these people bother about the abysmal quality of the town's roads when they don't have to drive over them?' Khobal was known for saying during tea breaks in the courts.

But Khobal's real claim to fame was as the lawyer who had got a death sentence in 2004 for the daughter and son-in-law of Relu Ram, an independent legislator from Barwala in Hisar district, who, along with seven other family members, had been hacked to death a few years ago. It was a sensational killing, which had sent shock waves across North India. Relu Ram's nineteen-year-old daughter and her husband were arrested for the crime, and they had admitted that they committed the murders to become the sole owners of her father's fabulous property. In February 2007 the Supreme Court had upheld the death sentence awarded by the Hisar sessions court and Khobal was basking in the glow of his achievement. He was at that time also handling a case relating to the rape and murder of a nine-year-old girl and had begun to be counted among the foremost criminal lawyers in Hisar.

It had been a long and hard journey for him. Son of a farmer from Prabhuwala village, some forty-five kilometres from Hisar, he had made many sacrifices along the way. He was the only one among his five brothers who had gone beyond Class X, enrolling later for his bachelor's degree in law. His mother believes that his name has much to do with the fame coming his way. He was named Lal Bahadur by his grandfather because he was born on the day Prime Minister Lal Bahadur Shastri died. The old man, a Congress politician, had gone to attend the prime minister's funeral in Delhi, and when he returned to find that a grandson had been born to him he pronounced, 'Lal Bahadur has returned in our family.'

To his credit, Lal Bahadur never forgot his humble beginnings. Ever since he began practising law in the district courts and made Hisar his home in 1991, he had been an active social worker and remained in touch with prominent social organizations and other non-governmental organizations (NGOs) of the area. This is how he had met Shakuntala Jakhar and, together, the two had helped many luckless women who often came to them for help. But when Shakuntala broached the subject of Chandrapati's case in the Karnal court and how she needed a good lawyer to represent her, Lal Bahadur refused point-blank. 'Shakuntalaji, it will not be possible for me to take up this case. It has already acquired a high profile, with the powerful Jat khaps being involved.'

Shakuntala conveyed Lal Bahadur's refusal to Seema and said, 'Don't worry, we'll find someone else to fight your case.'

That night, Lal Bahadur discussed the offer with Trishna and she supported his decision not to take it up. 'Just forget it ji. We are no match for these Jats who have powerful people backing them. Besides, where is it written that you have to fight every murder case that comes to your doorstep?'

'That's what I was thinking. The family is also very poor. I doubt if they can even give me a decent fee. It will involve going to Karnal every other day for hearings, the expense of frequent travel and, then, what about the Jat khaps? I think I'll avoid Shakuntala for a few days so that she doesn't get a chance to bring up the subject again.'

Long after Trishna had gone to sleep, Lal Bahadur mulled over the issue. The Relu Ram case had been a piece of cake because not only was there plenty of evidence from the scene of crime, he also had the support of people across the state, who were incensed by the murders. Many a time during the trial, he had felt like a heroic warrior vanquishing evil, and wherever he went people lauded him for it. 'If I take up this Chandrapati woman's case, I will be pitted against the might of the state. The same people who praised me will hurl abuses. No, I had better not do anything foolhardy,' he thought, his mind turning to his two daughters sleeping in the other room. 'Trishna is right.'

Two days later, as he entered his office after arguing a case in court, he found Seema and Chandrapati waiting for him. He had never met them before but guessed it was them because he had seen their photographs in many newspapers.

'Lal Bahadurji, we want you to fight our case. Shakuntalaji must have spoken to you about it. Please don't refuse us,' said Seema.

Fighting off the irritation he felt on seeing them, Lal Bahadur forced himself to be polite. 'Did Shakuntala not tell you that I don't have the time for your case right now? I am busy with another rape-cum-murder matter and all my assistants have their hands full at this time.'

Chandrapati pulled her chair closer to his desk. 'Sirji, we are very needy. We have heard about your competence and know that only you will be able to help us in this matter. Don't worry about the fee, we will arrange whatever you want.'

'It's not possible. I cannot help you. I can suggest another colleague who is also very able. If you say, I will talk to him for you,' said Lal Bahadur and began gathering his papers to indicate that he had to go for another hearing.

She still doesn't know what it was, but that first visit to his office convinced Seema that he was the lawyer for them. They spent the night in a room above the JMS's small office in Hisar, which Shakuntala had arranged for them, and tried to meet him again the next day. But Lal Bahadur had gone to Chandigarh on some work and did not return till late in the evening. The two women decided to go home and try another day. In the following days, Seema called him every other day. Sometimes she caught a bus and reached his Hisar office to personally press her case. By now Lal Bahadur was beginning to get amused by the girl's tenacity and one day, when she called him in the evening, he said that his fee would be very high and they would find it hard to pay him.

'Just name a figure, sir. We will sell or mortgage our land and raise the money. But we want justice for Manoj and Babli,' said Seema.

'After the Relu Ram case my fee has gone up. I will charge two lakh rupees and another fifty thousand for travelling expenses from Hisar to Karnal and back, during the trial,' said Lal Bahadur, quite sure that the huge sum quoted by him would effectively end the nuisance. 'Theek hai, sir,' said Seema and Lal Bahadur smiled.

'They will not bother me now,' he thought.

Just before noon the next day, Seema was back. As soon as she entered, she reached for his table to put a packet containing currency notes on it. 'This is twenty-five thousand rupees, sir. The first instalment of your fees. We will give you the rest as the case progresses.'

Two of his junior colleagues were in the office and were watching. They all knew how Seema and Chandrapati had been pursuing Lal Bahadur for the last many days and wondered what he would do now. 'I did not mean that you should bring the money so soon, Seema. But let me consult my juniors also, before I finally take up your case,' he hedged.

That evening, Lal Bahadur's five junior assistants surprised him by insisting that he should not refuse the case any more. 'Let's accept this case as a challenge, sir. The family is helpless but they seem to be very brave. I think we should do it,' said the most junior.

'Dekh lo bhai, if there is trouble during the trial, then don't blame me. This is no ordinary murder case. Powerful politicians are behind the accused and they can physically harm us,' Khobal warned.

He could see that the consensus in his office was against him and he now had the task of convincing his wife. Trishna still had reservations but reluctantly agreed to let him go ahead with it. 'Perhaps it is in his destiny. Who knows, some good might come out of it,' she told herself.

*

The slugfest between the left organizations and the Jat Mahasabha over the failure of the police to arrest Gangaraj had intensified. The trial had begun in a Karnal court but only the six other accused were being tried.

In Rohtak's Jasbir Colony, the JMS activists were chalking out plans for yet another protest on the Gangaraj issue. Shakuntala had come over from Hisar and their Kaithal district president, Anu Prashar, too had been summoned. They sat around a bare table which had not seen polish for years. Piles of dusty newspapers sat on the floor and a couple of shelves held an assortment of much-thumbed files containing petitions, memorandums, newspaper clippings and more. Someone ordered a round of tea and a barefooted boy from the tea stall leaning against their office wall brought small glasses of the sweet brew. Jagmati took a sip and tucked an errant lock of her hair into her single plait. Pulling up her chair to the table, she took out a sheet of paper from her purse. 'Anu has compiled a list of the public events at which Gangaraj's presence has been reported by newspapers. It's quite obvious that unless the pressure is stepped up the police will not arrest him.'

'I spoke to Chandrapati this morning. She was telling me that people in the village still don't talk to them openly. She thinks it is only a matter of time before someone attacks Vinod or Seema,' said Anu.

'I've discussed the matter with our leaders in Delhi. We are going ahead with our plan to hold a street protest in Karnal. You will all have to mobilize as much support as you can to make it an impressive event,' said Jagmati.

Shakuntala nodded. 'We can get banners printed from our usual vendor. I have also asked some college girls to make placards. Anu, you check if Seema and Chandrapati can join the protest.'

'Hmmm. Seema usually comes home from Jaipur on weekends. I'll call and ask if she can go back a day late. It is important that she and her mother be present. It will galvanize the workers,' said Anu.

On 27 October the JMS and many other organizations took out a massive procession from Karan Park in Karnal and sat in dharna outside the camp office of Balkar Singh, deputy commissioner, Karnal. The protesters raised slogans, while Jagmati, Shakuntala, Premchand and a few others forced their way in and gheraoed the deputy commissioner. Seema and Chandrapati watched somewhat bemusedly. They had never even participated in a protest demonstration before, let alone been the central players. They struggled to do what was expected of them. Raise a slogan? Seema was shy. The activists around her wanted to hand over a memorandum to press for Gangaraj's arrest, but the irate official was in no mood to humour them. The Gangaraj fracas had been getting on his nerves for the last few weeks, with not only Manoj's family petitioning him for his arrest but the media also being at his throat. And now these strident, loud-mouthed women were muscling their way into his office.

He knew that he did not have much of a say in this matter. It had been made clear to him by officials in the Haryana government secretariat in Chandigarh that he should 'know what are the stakes and handle the matter accordingly'. After being in the civil service for more than a decade, he knew what that meant and he, for one, was not going to stick his neck out.

Seeing Jagmati and her gang barging in, he squarely scolded them. Jagmati scarcely heard him. 'We are not going from here today until Gangaraj is arrested. This is the height of irresponsibility. There is no rule of law in this state.' Some activists began raising slogans behind her and the office staff abandoned their files and tea to watch the spectacle.

'This is sheer hooliganism. I will not tolerate it. You are obstructing the work of a government official and can be prosecuted for it.'

The women around his table were enraged. 'Okay. Arrest us all then. That should be easier for you than arresting Gangaraj,' said Shakuntala.

'Yes, yes, do it. That is all that impotent officials like you can do,' said another woman. But Chandrapati was unable to say anything. There was something about a government office that made her normally feisty self freeze. She had seen it happening to her again and again. Overwhelmed by the deputy commissioner's office, she pulled helplessly at her dupatta and stood grimly in a corner. The Karnal demonstration was widely covered by the vernacular newspapers, and Jat organizations took note of it with concern.

A few days later Jagmati advised Seema that they should also meet the state's director general of police, Ranjiv Singh Dalal, to press for Gangaraj's arrest. She herself called up the DGP's office to fix up an appointment and on the appointed day Seema, Chandrapati and Narinder accompanied her to the police headquarters at Panchkula. They had come prepared with a memorandum to present him, but to their disappointment Dalal was not there to meet them. Jagmati was unusually sharp with the clerk in his office. 'What is this? Your sahib has given us time for today. He should have had the decency to be present.'

'Madam, sahib had to go for an urgent meeting. Please accept apologies on his behalf. If you so desire, you can meet the IG law and order. He will listen to your problem.'

'Okay. Now that we have come from so far, we might as well meet someone. We have to hand over this memorandum,' she said. The other three said very little. The place exuded power. They were awed into silence. Seema fiddled with her dupatta, using its corner to wipe the sweat on her upper lip, as she usually did when nervous. Chandrapati's face wore the implacable expression it assumed in front of authority. But Jagmati's ire was roused and by the time they entered the office of the inspector general she was raring to go. It was a short and sharp exchange.

'This is our memorandum for the DGP. Your force has still not arrested Gangaraj, though he roams around all over the state with impunity. What kind of law and order is this?' she began.

The officer's jaw tightened. 'This is an issue which has arisen from an intra-gotra marriage. As you know, such transgressions are not tolerated in any Hindu society. Repercussions will be there.'

'Sir, this is a case of cold-blooded murder. The reasons could be anything, gotra or anything else. You are bound by the law to arrest the accused. Even if society has sanctioned the murders, your law has not,' she said, uncharacteristically loud. Again Chandrapati was tongue-tied.

But Seema could see it was quite hopeless. She tugged at Jagmati's arm and whispered, 'Behenji, let's go. It's no use arguing with him. Just give him the memorandum.' They handed over their carefully prepared piece of paper. It had lain in Seema's folder of documents throughout their bus journey from Kaithal to Panchkula. Now the folded paper, which to Seema looked somewhat soiled amid the sparkling stationery on his table, lay forlorn in the centre of the table. The IG picked it up and put it in a drawer. 'I will give it to DGP sahib. *Aur kuchh?*'

The foursome walked out in disgust.

World Human Rights Day falls on 10 December, and in 2007 the JMS, DYFI and other organizations that had participated in the Karnal protest held a similar demonstration outside Jantar Mantar in Delhi and submitted a memorandum before the National Human Rights Commission. They demanded that:

1. The Haryana police arrest all the guilty persons including Gangaraj as he was obviously directly involved with the murder of Manoj and Babli.
2. The State government be directed to provide protection to Manoj's family and ensure that no boycott, including any hindrance in the education of Manoj's brother Vinod, continues.
3. The State government immediately provide compensation to Manoj's family and help them economically.
4. The guilty police personnel, who colluded with Babli's family and acted against the couple and Manoj's family and later delayed the investigation, be punished.

*

Incensed by all this, the All India Adarsh Jat Mahasabha felt it was time to give a fitting reply, one that would deliver a solid punch on the nose.

They decided to honour Gangaraj with the Jat Gaurav (pride of Jats) award. On a bitterly cold December day, hundreds of men from across Haryana gathered at the Jat Dharamsala in Kurukshetra to attend a Jat Chintan Shivir or Jat introspection camp where Gangaraj was to be honoured. The aim was twofold: to send a message to the political powers that the sabha was with Gangaraj and any attempt to arrest him would invite retaliation from the community; and also to convey to the left organizations that their efforts were futile.

Many journalists from the local Kurukshetra press also turned up. They looked forward to reporting the open defiance of the law by the Jat panchayats and some even made video recordings of the event. Pavanjit Banwala did the honours at the function, where Gangaraj was garlanded and presented with a memento and shawl for upholding the values of Jat society.

Just as he ascended the stage, a voice from the audience shouted, 'Isn't he the one?' Gangaraj whirled around. A supporter shouted, *'Na, na, na, yeh toh bahut . . .'* but a beaming Gangaraj raised a hand and said, *'Rehne do, bhai.'* Throughout the function, there was a self-righteous smirk on his face and he kept glancing appreciatively at the crowd seated behind him. The reporters, however, were disappointed at his not giving an acceptance speech.

Jaipal Dhand of *Amar Ujala* frowned. 'We'll have to check if he has refused to talk from the stage or whether the organizers did not ask him at all. It's not like him to give up such an opportunity.'

'I think he's just scared to open his mouth now. He knows we are all here just to report on him,' added a reporter.

'Have you noticed he has a fixed smile on his face? The charge sheet must be worrying him. For how long will the government continue to bail him out? The pressure is building up,' whispered Jaipal.

They sat up with interest when Banwala began speaking. He delivered a chilling speech in which he brazenly asserted that those who married in the same gotra would meet the fate of Manoj and Babli. Another khap leader said the others who had joined Gangaraj in his noble task would be honoured whenever they were released from jail.

A few speakers demanded that the government should discourage intra-caste marriages by declaring them illegal. A demand also came up to scrap the Special Marriage Act, 1954, which gives legitimacy to such mismatched marriages. Among those present were the national president of the Jat Mahasabha, Birender Singh; former MLA Udhai Singh; president of the Nain and Bawal khaps, Nafe Singh Nain; president of the formidable Meham Chaubisi khap, Surat Singh; Ishwar Singh of Rohtak 85 panchayat; and Omkar Singh of Sonepat 360 panchayat. All the major Jat outfits of Haryana were represented that day.

But the journalists who had hoped for a juicy story and some more sound bites from this controversial leader of the Jats went home disappointed. Gangaraj did not speak a word publicly and went out of his way to avoid them. Kamal Midha, a stringer for CNN-IBN, trained his cameras on him when he came out of hall, and chased him, in vain, till Gangaraj left the premises. The burly flunkey who accompanied him was ready to prevent pesky media people from approaching him. Kamal's last shot of Gangaraj shows him looking furtively over his shoulder as he is picking his way through the crowds.

*

These were heady days for Gangaraj. He was being feted for his role in the Manoj–Babli case, the police was scared to touch him and the man himself revelled in his seeming invincibility. This is perhaps why the principal of Karoran Government Senior Secondary School chose to invite him and the sarpanch Karambir as the chief guests for the school's Republic Day function on 26 January 2008.

At home, sixteen-year-old Vinod, all excited, was preparing for the occasion. 'Ma, I have stood first in class and will be given a prize today,' he told Chandrapati. Vinod is everything that Manoj was not: bright as well as good at sports. Though the youngest and most pampered in the family, he had, after the tragedy that had befallen the family, suddenly become responsible. Chandrapati was paranoid about his security. In one of her rare gestures of affection, she caressed his head. *'Mera lal, ja kuch accha baniyo.'* Son, go and do well in life.

He touched her feet before rushing out. She stifled the urge to hug him. He looked so fine in his blue shirt and khaki pants and so happy. 'God, I hope no evil eye falls on him,' she thought.

Vinod had barely entered the school gate when his only friend, Santosh, told him that Gangaraj was to be the chief guest that day. The boy's face fell. There was hardly a day when the family did not discuss the reluctance of the police to arrest him. Their after-dinner conversations around the kitchen fire were almost always about Gangaraj. He had, in many ways, become their enemy number 1, the Ravana who had robbed them of their happiness.

Standing in the queue, waiting to receive his prize, Vinod hoped that Karambir, not Gangaraj, would be called to give away the prizes, but there was no such luck. 'Please welcome Gangaraj Karoran, a distinguished leader of our village,' the principal was saying.

Vinod looked at the man's beaming face. 'What an ignominy for me! I don't want this prize from him. What if I quietly walk away from here? No one will notice. Or better still, should I walk up to the stage and give him a slap? That will really make them all sit up. The press will report it and the police will have to come and arrest him . . .'

All this rushed through his mind, even as his name was called out by someone on stage. His feet took him up. His hands stretched out for the commendation certificate. All he could do was glower at Gangaraj, before walking away. If anyone noticed his rage that day, they did not talk about it. But it was framed for posterity in the photograph that the school photographer took of Vinod receiving the prize.

His elation at getting a prize had evaporated. In its place was an alien, leaden feeling, as if he had been bludgeoned with a bag of cement. Vinod did not wait to talk to anyone in school after the function and rushed home to share his mortification with the family. The photograph which he received a few days later was stored by Chandrapati in her trunk. They knew it was no use showing it to the police as proof that Gangaraj was very much in the village and that they should come and arrest him. It was to remain a souvenir of their ultimate humiliation.

*

On 10 March 2008, some six months after the first charge sheet was submitted before the court, the State Crime Branch (SCB) at Madhuban (which was now investigating the case) submitted a supplementary charge sheet naming Gangaraj as an accused under Sections 364, 302, 201 and 120 B of the IPC. The matter would come up before the illaqua magistrate, Karnal, Narinder Pal. It sent a frisson of anticipation in the prosecution's camp. Lal Bahadur and his juniors gathered at his modest house in Hisar's New Jawahar Colony to discuss the development late into the night. There was a twist in it.

'There is a provision under Section 173-8 of the CrPc, under which, if an accused is untraceable at the time of filing the charge sheet, the police can produce a supplementary charge sheet when the accused is taken into custody. But in this case, they have submitted the supplementary charge sheet without arresting Gangaraj. This is ridiculous,' said Lal Bahadur.

'Sir, have you noticed the charge sheet mentions that Gangaraj had appeared before the SCB Madhuban with his lawyer on 29 February. They just questioned him and let him go! They should have arrested him then and there,' said Surat Singh.

'Rajesh, just read that bit again for everyone,' said Lal Bahadur.

The young lawyer, fresh out of law school, was excited at handling his first major case. He began reading from a copy of the charge sheet before him.

'On 29/2/2007 after much effort, Gangaraj along with his lawyer appeared at the SCB office in Madhuban. During questioning, he said that his mobile phone with number 94165 63752 had got lost and he asked for time to prove his innocence. However, he did not appear on the date given to him. The police though, already had details of his mobile phone conversation and also records to show that this phone belonged to him, from Surender Kumar deputy general manager BSNL, Ambala circle. His letter certifying this is attached with this charge sheet.'

There was a moment of silence as everyone digested the information. Surat went out to the patio to take a call. Yogesh shifted in his chair. 'We should draw the attention of the press to this. Let them haul these khaki bastards over the coals.'

Lal Bahadur smiled. 'The press can read and figure it out for themselves. It won't help our case in any way. We have to concentrate on building up our evidence and ensure that nothing gets derailed or sabotaged during the trial. God knows there is plenty of mischief afoot.'

'The police could have declared him a proclaimed offender, when he did not turn up on the date given to him at Madhuban. That would have been the right thing to do in a normal case.'

Surat came in. 'The magistrate has fixed 18 March to accept the charge sheet. Let's see if he questions the police about why they have not taken Gangaraj into custody.'

On the 18th Lal Bahadur had to appear before the Hisar sessions judge in another case, so he deputed Yogesh and Surat to attend the proceedings in the Karnal illaqua magistrate's court.

The SCB appeared to be prepared for the judicial magistrate Narinder Pal's (designated as illaqua magistrate) queries. As soon as Pal asked DSP Puran Chand about the absence of Gangaraj, he submitted a statement. It read:

> This is to state that a supplementary charge sheet has been presented in this court against accused Gangaraj, without arresting him because we apprehend that his arrest can lead to a law and order problem. In view of this, I have presented this charge sheet without taking him into custody, so that further proceedings can take place.

Narinder Pal smiled. He had been following the case closely and knew all about the police's cat and mouse game with Gangaraj. He issued non-bailable warrants against Gangaraj and fixed 23 May as the next date by which the police was required to produce him.

The media went to town with the news.

The police still dithered. No officer wanted to carry out the unpleasant task of arresting Gangaraj. They all knew that the consequences could be harsh. The khaps had assumed a threatening stance. Besides, the chief minister's visit to Karoran in September had sent the message down the ranks.

On 23 May the SCB again cut a sorry figure before Narinder Pal as they had still not arrested the accused Gangaraj. Non-bailable warrants were issued once again with 7 July as the next date.

All this had caused a churning in Gangaraj's camp. Apparently, the Congress leadership was upset with the adverse media coverage it was getting over the Chandrapati case and the failure to arrest Gangaraj was becoming an embarrassment. DSP Puran Chand's statement about a potential law and order problem had made things worse. It made the government look weak and the police incompetent to handle a backlash. Gangaraj had begun getting feelers from Chandigarh to surrender.

Lal Bahadur heard of these developments from the court grapevine. 'Arre bhai, Lal Bahadur,' his long-time colleague Randhir Singh had called out when he went in for his mid-morning tea and samosas. 'That Gangaraj is going to surrender soon. You mark my words. Mantri sahib has told him that his case will be taken care of. But he should give himself up at this moment, so that the clamour against him quietens down.'

'Aapke muh mein ghee shakkar, Randhir sahib,' said Lal Bahadur smiling. He pulled a faded plastic chair close to his colleague and decided to order bread pakoras to go with his tea. *'Do bread pakore aur chai, Chajju,'* he called out to the canteen boy.

Turning towards Randhir, he said, 'How reliable is your information? I'm waiting for Gangaraj to be arrested. The case cannot proceed without him. What we are doing now is a waste of time.'

'My information is hundred per cent true. It's from Congress circles and they are quite worried.'

Lal Bahadur looked at him doubtfully. He knew that Randhir was a keen Congress supporter and used to hobnob with party biggies. During the last assembly elections he had lobbied for a party ticket from Ellenabad but had lost out to the local moneybags, who according to the grapevine had paid off people in Delhi to get the seat. Randhir had taken to bad-mouthing his favourite party after this. His not getting a ticket was a standing joke in the Hisar courts. But in the last six months he had got three briefs from prominent Congress leaders. Lal Bahadur was not sure what his present equation with the party leadership was. He finished his tea and pakoras and pushed back his chair.

Randhir Singh burped. He had downed one plate of chana bhatura and had started on a plate of dark gulab jamuns swimming in sugar syrup. 'If Gangaraj surrenders, you will have your hands full. I can see that coming.'

Lal Bahadur had learned not to disregard canteen gossip. 'However unreliable it might be, there is always a kernel of truth somewhere,' he told himself. Mentally filing away the information, he walked out into the shade of several old neem trees around the court complex.

*

On 28 March Pavanjit Banwala and his All India Adarsh Jat Mahasabha raised the pitch some more. He called a few journalists of Kaithal to the Jat School lawns and, over tea and jalebis specially ordered for them, delivered a categorical message for the politicos. 'We are submitting a memorandum to the director general of state police and the deputy commissioner of Kaithal on Saturday in which we shall make it clear that if Gangaraj is arrested the Jat organizations will rise in revolt and the administration will be responsible for what follows.' He warned that hundreds of people from the mahasabha, its workers and office-bearers, and villagers of Karoran were ready to be arrested in place of Gangaraj. 'The charge sheet submitted by the State Crime Branch, Madhuban, is based on wrong facts and inferences. It is unfortunate that the court has issued non-bailable warrants against him based on these wrong facts. We are going to hold Jat panchayats across the state in the coming days to chalk out the next plan of action and also to deliberate on how best to fight this court case,' he finished. The scribes scribbled furiously into their notebooks but did not forget to tuck into the sweets. His exertions went waste because, a few days after Banwala's talk with the journalists, Gangaraj surrendered before the court of the illaqua magistrate, who sent him to judicial custody. In other words, to jail.

*

Lal Bahadur and his team held another brainstorming session. It was in his cabin in the Hisar district courts complex. Though it wasn't the best place for serious deliberation, with litigants walking in and out and some hanging about outside, they needed to take immediate stock of the situation. Gangaraj's surrender necessitated a change of tack.

By now, the trial in the Karnal district court had commenced and the prosecution had already recorded the evidence of four witnesses including Narinder and Kuldeep. Lal Bahadur and his team were now wholeheartedly into the controversial case and everyone in the Hisar court knew that he had taken it up. It made him feel good. His long years of struggle had taught him to give his everything to whatever he attempted. His initial reluctance to take up the matter had given way to enthusiastic preparations and he found that his juniors too were devoting considerable time to discussing its finer aspects.

He ran his fingers through his thinning hair and made a mental note to henna it on the weekend. All this running back and forth to Karnal had left him with barely any time for himself. If he had his way, he was going to put the trial on hold for some time. At least till the charges against Gangaraj were framed.

'We have to change our strategy. With Gangaraj's arrest the whole case is transformed. Our attention should be diverted towards the charges against him,' he addressed his team.

'That's true. Gangaraj's counsel has made it clear that they would like to argue the charges against him and will not accept the police charge sheet as it is. This means that we have a two-pronged battle on our hands. The ongoing trial in the Karnal sessions court and now a parallel matter regarding the charges,' said Lt Col (retd) Om Prakash. He had retired from the army's Judge Advocate-General (JAG) branch a few years ago and Lal Bahadur valued his sagacity and presence in the team. They all turned to listen to him. 'We already have the testimonies of four witnesses, and if we allow the trial to proceed normally, whenever charges are framed against Gangaraj, the witnesses will have to testify all over again.'

'Then it makes sense for us to stop the ongoing trial and wait for charges to be framed against Gangaraj. If we don't do this, the case will drag on for years. Who knows how many witnesses will be compromised in that time? A quick trial always favours the prosecution, in such matters,' said Lal Bahadur, voicing a concern that was beginning to play on the minds of others in the room by now. 'It's quite clear that they want to buy time and God knows what else. We'll match them move for move.

'When is the next date, Surat? Call up the district attorney and inform him that we are not going to produce any more witnesses for evidence until the judge frames charges against Gangaraj. And, on the next hearing, we will all go together to the court to inform the judge of this,' said Lal Bahadur with finality.

For the next few months the Manoj–Babli murder trial in the Karnal sessions court came to a virtual halt as Gangaraj and his defence counsel challenged the police charge sheet. Outside the courtroom though, there was plenty of action and drama.

*

Premchand and his associates were supposed to be rehearsing a play in the veranda of the DYFI office in Kaithal, and had gathered here as they did every week for this. Today, however, no one's heart was in it. Instead, the motley group of activists and artists huddled together for a discussion which continued late into the evening. Titled *Inhen Jeene Do* (Let them live), their street play was part of the public campaign they were mounting against honour killings, illegal diktats by khaps and other social evils like female feticide and dowry. Three days ago, they had staged the play in Deban village, sixteen kilometres from Kaithal on the Jind road. The in-laws of one of their activists, Yogesh, lived there and he had offered to arrange lodging for them to stay overnight. Unlike other villages, where such street plays with social messages did not attract much attention, here a decent crowd had gathered to watch and the activists put up a spirited performance. When the play finished and they were winding up, a handful of village goons confronted them and demanded to know who had given them permission to put up the play here.

Premchand assumed his best placatory tone. 'This is a street play, bhaiyo. It can be shown anywhere. We have not hired your chaupal for this purpose, because for us even the shade of a tree is enough to spread the message.'

'Keep your message to yourself. It is not needed in this village. Do you understand? And we don't want to see any of you here again.' To show that they meant business, the goons began to push and shove the activists, who quickly left the venue. They had spent an uneasy night in the village, and made a quiet exit as soon as day broke.

But the incident was bothering Premchand. He asked Yogesh to conduct a discreet inquiry into what had provoked this reaction against them. Some of the activists were unnerved and the parents of a girl had refused to allow her to participate in any more of their productions. He had to get to the bottom of this.

Yogesh walked into their evening huddle purposefully. They all turned towards him expectantly. He squatted on a pile of bricks. 'I have found out what the problem is. You won't believe this,' he began. 'I have been told that at least four honour killings have taken place in this Deban village alone and all of them were hushed up. No one, neither the police nor the media, got wind of the killings; it's the village's collective secret. The reasons are the usual ones. Either the girls ran away with boys from the lower castes or married into a bhaichara gotra. This is why they were opposing our play. There is an army man from the village who married a girl from his bhaichara gotra a few years ago and till today they have not let him enter the village. If he comes, he will surely be killed,' said Yogesh. They listened in silence.

Premchand sensed that some of the boys and girls had

become nervous. 'Chalo, these are the kinds of hurdles we should learn to expect. After all, the opposition to our play has shown that the problem is deep-rooted and we have to work harder to rid our society of it,' he said.

He decided to share a telephone conversation he had had with an official from the office of the Chief Judicial Magistrate (CJM) that morning. It would cheer them up.

'In this ruckus, I forgot to tell you that there has been one positive outcome of our play. As you know, some of our performances in the other villages have received appreciative media coverage. The chief minister and chief justice of the Punjab and Haryana High Court are scheduled to visit Kaithal next month and the CJM has asked whether we can show our play at that function. He has seen a news report about our play.' An immediate buzz went through the group and Premchand smiled. He was scheduled to meet the CJM, D.S. Parmar, the next day and asked Yogesh and a couple of others to accompany him to the court complex.

Their meeting with the CJM did not go as anticipated. Parmar was keen to have their group perform before the chief minister but with one condition. 'Remove the bits about khaps and honour killings and focus instead on dowry and female feticide,' he told them. 'We have read about your plays and the people seem to like them, but see if you can change it a little to suit our function.' This was most unexpected. The DYFI guys were taken aback.

'Sir, none of our plays are without references to honour crimes. It's not possible to remove them. We are doing these plays for a cause, not for commercial gains,' Premchand patiently explained to the magistrate. His argument did not impress Parmar one bit and the official stuck to his condition.

On their way back Premchand was ruminating that

perhaps Parmar's condition was not so unexpected after all. He should have been prepared for it. 'The judicial officer too comes from the society that has the same mindset as the complicit policemen. A voice raised against this crime was bound to make him uncomfortable,' he said.

'Ditto for the chief minister and his Jat colleagues. It won't do to have a street play about honour crimes in his presence. Parmar will get a rap on the knuckles if he does that. Haven't we seen the CM's support for khaps in the Manoj–Babli case?' said Yogesh.

Premchand shook his head and laughed. 'How foolish of us to think that we could perform *Inhen Jeene Do* before them. Forget it, guys. Let's go home.'

*

Jaipur was hot at this time of the year. Gusts of loo winds howled about Seema's PG digs the whole afternoon. The loo hadn't let up even when she walked back from college a little later. She was tired and the sandy grit in her hair was beginning to irritate. Her two room-mates had gone shopping for groceries, so she decided to get down to prepare for the next day's class assignment. But, try as she might, she just couldn't concentrate on the textbook on the Indian Penal Code in front of her. Her head ached. Rekha normally called every evening to update her on the latest news in Karoran. But today when the cell phone rang, she wished she could ignore the call. Rekha sounded excited on the line.

'Narinder was telling us that the Haryana police is filling up vacancies for constables and has invited applications. Ma wants you to try for it, Seema.'

'*Accha?* I am already busy with this law course. I haven't had time to study for these exams this year—how will I prepare for the police test? It's quite tough,' she replied wearily. It seemed as if nothing could uplift her spirits. She was just so tired of everything and wanted to be left alone. 'What's wrong with me? Am I falling ill?' she wondered, as she disconnected the call. The news of the police recruitment had not excited her one bit. For the next two days, she mulled over her mother's message. She knew how important it was for her to get a job. After Manoj's death, their financial situation had become quite desperate. The court case was eating up all their savings and it was becoming difficult to pay Vinod's school fees. With the boycott against them still lingering, she wasn't even sure if they would be able to contract their land for a decent price this year. But she did not want to become a police constable. Not again.

In 2004 she had dropped her BA second-year exams to avail of a similar police recruitment drive. Om Prakash Chautala of the Indian National Lok Dal (INLD) was the chief minister and he had raised the Haryana State Industrial Security Force for which 3500 jawans were being recruited. It was an election year and the ruling party was dishing out government jobs to build up a loyal constituency ahead of the elections. Consequently, most of the vacancies were filled with candidates recommended by INLD office-bearers. Seema was one of them and her candidature had been recommended by the Kaithal district president of the INLD. But the very next year, when Chautala went out of power, one of the first steps of Bhupinder Singh Hooda's Congress government was to disband the force. Seema lost her job and had no choice but to restart her studies. She finished her graduation from Pundri and was now taking this course in Jaipur.

'I haven't enrolled for a law course so that I should become a lowly constable. If I clear all the papers, I can become a lawyer or, better still, a judge,' she thought.

Nevertheless, on her next visit to Karoran, she filled the

form and began to prepare for the police test. It was no use wishing for the moon. For the moment, it was important to get a job. Any job, to keep the home fires burning. Rekha had dropped out of school a couple of years ago and Vinod was still too young. It fell on her, Seema, to shoulder the family's responsibilities. But she promised herself that one day she would follow her heart.

As luck would have it, she failed the physical test at the Yamunanagar police grounds because she was unable to run as fast as the other girl candidates. It was a huge disappointment. Chandrapati shared it with Shakuntala and Anu when the two went to look her up one day. They, in turn, informed Jagmati in Rohtak and the ever-helpful JMS ladies began to apply their minds on how to get Seema the job she so badly needed.

*

In the first week of September 2008, something unexpected happened. The media missed its import, but the ears of those in the know, like Lal Bahadur and his team, pricked up. Surat had gone to Karnal to appear before the court of Additional Sessions Judge Bant Prakash, which was considering the framing of fresh charges against Gangaraj. He expected it would be a routine hearing, where the court would agree to give another date, as had been the case in the last few hearings and was looking forward to getting back to Hisar for lunch. The defence was supposed to be arguing on the framing of charges, but so far Surat had seen no progress on this. It was just one date after another, on different pretexts. He was looking absent-mindedly at the papers on his lap and almost didn't hear Bant Prakash's announcement that he would not be presiding over this trial any more. 'How odd,' thought Surat. 'What could have provoked the judge to recuse himself from the case?'

A written statement pronounced in open court said:

> On account of certain personal reasons, I do not deem it proper to conduct the trial of this case. The file is ordered to be placed before learned District and Sessions Judge, Karnal, with the request to transfer the same to some other court of competent jurisdiction. Parties are directed to appear before learned District and Sessions Judge, Karnal, on 5.9.2008 at 10 am. Accused who are in custody, also be produced before learned District and Sessions Judge.

Lunch forgotten, Surat spent the rest of the day trying to find out what could have happened to make Bant Prakash withdraw from the case. He couldn't unearth much.

The very next day, Vinod Jain, sessions judge of Karnal, transferred the case to the court of Additional Sessions Judge Balbir Singh. All the seven accused in custody, Mandeep Singh, Gurdev Singh, Suresh Kumar, Rajinder Sigh, Satish Kumar, Baru Ram and Gangaraj, were present in the courtroom. They looked on impassively.

Back in Hisar, the news had spread to the district courts there. Senior lawyers nodded and opined that judges usually recused themselves from a case if a relative was a party in the matter or if he had been threatened or 'approached' by either side to give a decision favouring them.

At their evening conference in Lal Bahadur's house, the team pondered over the development. 'Remember, I told you all that there is something at play behind the decision of Gangaraj's counsel to argue on charges against him. They just wanted to delay the framing of charges so that they could approach the judge in the meantime.'

'You mean he would have diluted the charges?' said Rajesh.

'No. That's for the police to decide and it would have to be done before submitting the charge sheet before the court. But the judge can drop the charges altogether if he finds there is no prima facie evidence to support them. In that case the matter against Gangaraj would have ended at this stage itself and he would have been discharged.'

'So what do you think has happened?'

'It's quite obvious that Bant Prakash was not willing to do their bidding. He has either been threatened or they tried to bribe him. The very fact that he quietly opted out means that he wants to avoid a controversy or a confrontation with them.'

'So what's next now?'

Lal Bahadur paused to take a sip of tea. 'Now that their tactics have been exposed, if they approach the next judge, it will be difficult for him to oblige. So we can look forward to charges being framed against Gangaraj. The trial will resume soon after that.' He shifted the teacups on the table to make place for the snacks which Trishna was bringing in.

*

The ancestral house of the Haryana chief minister Bhupinder Singh Hooda is a corner sprawl in Rohtak's D Park, Model Town. By its outer wall is a row of shops and the entrance is through a narrow lane. Even when the chief minister is not in town, the place is swarming with party workers, relatives and petitioners. It's an open house as befits a senior politician, and his wife, Asha Hooda, manages the hospitality. She has an imposing presence, a moonlike face, almost always adorned with a huge bindi and a matching smile. A few years into her husband's innings as chief minister, she was appointed vice president of the State Council for Child Welfare. It enables her to dabble in social work and oversee the implementation of government schemes for children and women.

Jagmati and her band of women gathered at the corner of the lane which leads into the house. It was a weighty delegation comprising Subha, Shakuntala, Sheela, Savita and Jagmati herself. Since they had reached Model Town from different directions—Shakuntala and Sheela came straight from Hisar—they held a small corner meeting to discuss how they should present their case. The agenda was a job for Seema in the Haryana police. There had been a consensus about this at their weekly meeting last Saturday. Seema had taken a bus from Kaithal to join them and now she nervously fingered the folder of documents in her hand.

'I think we should just confine ourselves to the plight of Seema's family and how a job for her will keep the wolf from their door. We should avoid mention of the harassment by khaps and Gangaraj. It won't help,' said Jagmati.

'I agree. We should focus on Vinod and Rekha's education too, and how they have no earning member left in their family,' said Shakuntala. The others nodded as they walked into the lane.

They were pleasantly surprised to find themselves being ushered into the sitting room. In the courtyard outside, desultory party workers sat on charpoys; the elderly among them were taking turns to smoke from a hookah. Asha welcomed them in a turquoise salwar kameez, gold bangles on her wrists and the distinctive bindi in place. Jagmati introduced them all and gave her a small brief about the activities of the JMS. The talk then turned towards the plight of women in Haryana. Asha told them of her initiation into social work by her father-in-law, Chaudhary Ranbir Singh, thrice MP from Rohtak. Subha drew her attention towards Seema and how she had missed getting a job in the police. As planned, the women explained the hardships being faced by Chandrapati's family and the dire straits they were in financially, after the death of Manoj.

Asha gave them a patient hearing. She knew of the Manoj–Babli murders and did not comment when the JMS activists recounted the case and its impact on Manoj's family. The women were hoping that her apparent distress at the condition of women in Haryana would move her to come to Seema's rescue. Asha sent them away with the assurance that she would try her best and also speak to her husband about the matter. She gave Seema an affectionate hug and told her not to worry. There seemed to be hope.

They chatted excitedly as they made their way to the bus stop on the main road from where they would get a bus to their office. 'She seemed quite positive. If she wants, she can certainly pull it off,' exclaimed Shakuntala.

Jagmati had been quiet after they came out of the chief minister's house. 'After all the flak they have got for shielding Gangaraj, this is Hooda's chance to redeem himself. I think he will do it. It's an opportunity for him to show his humane side,' she reflected.

A few days later Seema received a call, asking her to appear for the next stage of the selection procedure. She was selected and, in May 2008, joined the Madhuban police training academy for a ten-month-long training, prior to being inducted into the Haryana police. Chandrapati thanked the gods in her alcove but did not share the news with her neighbours. It wasn't like the old times any more. The sounds of their joys and sorrows, triumphs and defeats were confined to their four walls, not heard outside for a long time to come.

*

Shakuntala hadn't seen her sister Sudesh, elder to her by five years, for many months. She was pleasantly surprised, therefore, when she saw Sudesh alighting from a car in front of their newly built house in Hisar's urban estate one morning. She rushed out to hug her and only then did she notice that Sudesh didi was accompanied not by her husband but a whole lot of men Shakuntala couldn't recognize. Suppressing her disquiet at their sight, she smiled and welcomed them into her modest sitting room.

Unlike Shakuntala, Sudesh had never been to school and was married off at a young age to a Jat farmer in Dhad village of Kaithal district. She was known in their family as the 'simple one' who knew very little of the world beyond her home and hearth. As she made tea for them in the kitchen, Shakuntala wondered uneasily what Didi was doing in the company of these men. They drank their tea noisily. A middle-aged man in a shirt and pant, who seemed to be the leader of the group, poured the tea into his saucer and slurped it. Shakuntala waited patiently.

Sudesh was the first to speak: 'Shakuntala, these people are from Jakholi village and have fixed the marriage of their son to a girl from our family. That will make them our relatives. They are in deep trouble and are telling me that you can help them.'

The name Jakholi was vaguely familiar. Where had she heard it?

The leader of the group cleared his throat and said, 'Behenji, we are the relatives of Baru Ram and Gurdev, who as you know are in jail for the murders of Manoj and Babli. We want you to help us to get them out of this case.'

Jakholi. Of course! She got it. Quizzically, she looked at her sister.

'You have a good equation with Chandrapati's family and they will do anything you say. The truth is that our relatives have nothing to do with the murders. They were planned by Gangaraj. They just did what he told them to do. And he had promised them that he would get bail for them and also get the case withdrawn. But he himself is in jail now. If you speak with Chandrapati, to withdraw the names of the people from Jakholi from the FIR, we shall be very grateful to you. It's the people of Karoran who did it. The Jakholi guys just got dragged into it. They were instigated.'

Shakuntala did not respond.

'Behenji, we are prepared to spend any amount to free our kin. If you say we will get a new office building constructed for your JMS in Hisar . . .'

She looked at him carefully. Then turned to the others and studied each one of them. It was their turn to wait.

She addressed her sister: 'Didi, you don't know of this case. It is a heinous crime, a double murder which has ruined the lives of an entire family. Even if someone from your family were involved in this case, I don't think I would have helped.'

'Behenji, it's all in your hands now. We have come to you with great hope.'

Shakuntala began clearing away the teacups and carried them into the kitchen. Sudesh followed her inside. 'I had no idea what these people wanted to talk to you about. They just told me that they have some important work with you and that I should introduce them to you,' she said.

Shakuntala smiled and hugged her sister. 'I wish I did not have to turn you away like this, but I am helpless. It's a matter of my principles.'

'I understand. My little sister is more grown up than me now.'

CHAPTER SEVEN

Alone in Their Moment of Victory

One day, Seema was slapped in the court. It wasn't a sharp smack on the cheek but more like a blow which sent her reeling into the balustrade. Her dupatta slid off her shoulders and, when she looked up, people could see the red finger marks on her skin. Suresh paused for a moment to view his handiwork, and in that instant Seema saw the triumphant look on his face. Almost at once the policemen accompanying him and the six others accused, here for the court hearing, grabbed his hands and steered them all towards and down the staircase and into the waiting police van to take them back to jail. Gurdev and Baru Ram were delighted. 'Bitch! That felt good. If she hadn't fallen, I would have taken another swipe at her,' muttered Suresh, once they were in the van.

By the time Seema collected herself to call up Lal Bahadur, who was still in the courtroom, the men were on their way back to Ambala jail with their minders. She had been summoned to the court to give evidence, but the defence counsel had opposed this, saying that she and Chandrapati should testify together. Lal Bahadur had asked her to wait outside while he talked to the reader about the date of the next hearing, when both would be required to appear. This was when Suresh, Gurdev and the others were making their way out of the courtroom, and as they passed near Seema Suresh seized the chance he had been waiting for. Even days after it happened, tears welled up in her eyes whenever she thought of the humiliating incident. The bodyguard provided by the Kaithal police had proved quite ineffectual. Perhaps he was taken by surprise. More likely, the presence of the Karnal police accompanying the accused made him complacent and he had been just plain negligent about his charge.

Lal Bahadur rushed out of the courtroom. Seeing the state she was in, he hurried to get her a glass of water. 'This is terrible. Even in custody they are so bold as to assault you in full public view. We must complain to the police.'

He drafted a complaint, made Seema sign it and together they took it to the small police post located in the premises of the Karnal district courts. The cops assured them that they would take action.

For many days after that, Seema, and sometimes Lal Bahadur too, kept checking with the cops as to what had been done, but they never got a satisfactory reply. One day, the cop on duty said to Seema, 'What can we do? You must have provoked them. That is why he attacked you. Murder matters are very sensitive and you should have been careful.' She seethed, but had learned that it was pointless arguing with policemen unwilling to act. They would blame the complainant. Hadn't she seen it happening so many times with them in Rajaund and Kaithal? Little had changed.

They all had just begun to feel a little secure. The family had police protection at home and also when they went out. All the accused had been arrested and the fear of the khaps had abated somewhat. Their neighbours in Karoran had also begun talking to them and it seemed as if life could become normal once again. Though just one slap, the sheer brazenness of it shook them out of their placid state. 'Ma, they will not leave us. He had the guts to attack me in front of so many people in the court. Think of what they can do to us here, when we don't have this police security,' said Seema, back at home that evening.

Vinod and Rekha had listened wide-eyed as she related the incident. Then Rekha began to cry. Seema was also sobbing into her dupatta. Tears of anger and desperation.

'Silly girls,' said their mother. 'Crying has never helped anyone. Now that we have come this far, the good Lord above will show us the way ahead too.' But she was worried too. 'Oh God, what else do you have in store for us?'

*

In Hisar, Lal Bahadur was also apprehensive. Though he had put up a brave front, the attack on Seema had unnerved him. He hadn't told anyone till then, but each time he appeared in court, the hostile glares he got from Gangaraj, Baru Ram and Suresh made him nervous. It was as if they were trying to send him a silent threat and Lal Bahadur always averted his eyes. He and his team kept up their businesslike approach in court, studied their papers when the defence was arguing and generally kept a low profile. It helped that Lal Bahadur was not given to histrionics while arguing, but he couldn't help noticing that the accused and their relatives and supporters, who sometimes appeared in the court, always tried to provoke him and his team, either by shouting loudly or just by the sheer strength of their numbers.

After Seema was slapped, he instructed his team to try a different route instead of the straight highway they usually took, whenever any of them had to go to Karnal. He also decided that going forward they would go together, as a team, to Karnal. There was safety in numbers.

He didn't know then, but his skills were to be tested in many more ways. This time, in his office at home, in Hisar. It was late in the evening and a carload of men got down in front of his gate. Only two of them came into his office and the one in kurta pyjama introduced himself as Gurdev's brother. 'Here it comes,' thought Lal Bahadur, nervously fingering the pen he had picked up from the pen stand.

Gurdev's brother had come with an offer. He wanted Lal Bahadur to use his influence with Chandrapati and Seema to work out a compromise. 'Bhai sahib, we don't want this court case. It was all the doing of these people from Karoran and my brother has been unnecessarily dragged into it. He is innocent. We are prepared to spend any amount, just get him out of this mess,' he said.

Perhaps his humble beginnings or his long years as a criminal lawyer have made him non-confrontational: Lal Bahadur is not sure which of them. When pushed into a corner, he rarely fights back or turns nasty. So when Gurdev's relatives began persuading him to give up his lawyer's honour code and accept their proposition, the frightened lawyer took a deep breath. *'Bhai sahib, main aapki baat samajhta hoon.* I understand but I am also helpless; the women are not prepared to compromise.'

'Dekh lo, vakil sahib. Aap jo kahoge, hum wahi karenge. Aap muh toh kholo.' We'll do what you want us to—just say the word.

The lawyer began looking for an opportunity to change the subject. 'Accha, tell me, how exactly are you related to Gurdev? Is he your real brother? How many brothers and sisters do you have?'

His visitors answered each of his questions. They explained in detail their family tree, and where Gurdev fitted in. No one noticed that Lal Bahadur had his hand under the table and was scribbling furiously on his palm.

This was valuable information, which he had been trying hard to get. Establishing the relationship of the accused with Babli and her family was one of the challenges before him in the trial and it was crucial in proving the motive for the murders. He thanked Providence for dropping this opportunity into his lap and, by the time the men from Jakholi took their leave, a smile was playing on his lips.

Some days later, Jitender Jhakhar, a fellow lawyer and acquaintance in the Hisar district courts, dropped into his office. The lawyer had come with a request from one Zile Singh, whom Lal Bahadur vaguely knew as a notary in the courts.

'*Bhai Lal Bahadur, ek request hai*. You are doing that Manoj–Babli case in which Gangaraj is an accused. His brother is Zile Singh, a notary in our court, and he is keen to talk to you. Don't say no, please. I have promised him that you will not refuse to talk to him.'

'Why will I not talk to him? *Kya baat kar rahe ho, Jitender?* He is a fellow lawyer and that makes him a colleague of sorts. He is welcome to talk to me whenever he wishes,' said the ever-affable Lal Bahadur. A few days later, when he was sitting in the court at Karnal, waiting for the proceedings to begin, Zile Singh, clad in a black lawyer's coat and trousers, came and sat next to him.

'Bhai sahib, Jitenderji must have spoken to you about me. As you know, Gangaraj is my brother. He has been falsely accused in this case, and we need your help to extricate him from this mess,' he began.

By now Lal Bahadur had become quite an expert at fobbing off such requests. No belligerence, no indignation, just a quiet expression of helplessness to do what was being asked of him was his perfected style. Many days later, Gangaraj's defence tried to prove through his mobile phone records that the phone which had been used extensively to make calls to the other accused and the policemen from the scene of the crime and around it on the day of the murders was not his. It so happened that, due to an error, BSNL had fed in Gangaram instead of Gangaraj as the owner of his mobile connection number 9416563752. Lal Bahadur's knowledge of Zile Singh's relationship with Gangaraj came in handy at this stage. Lal Bahadur and the prosecution procured the original application made by Gangaraj when he applied for the connection in 2005. It showed that Zile Singh had signed as the local reference and the ration card which was attached with the application was in the name of Gangaraj. The lawyer prides himself on this bit of smart sleuthing as it exposed the defence strategy, and as he told his colleagues later, 'They could not get any advantage from that ploy.'

*

It was a small victory. But a big setback was round the corner. In the first week of December 2008, Kuldeep was to depose before the court. A few days before that, Seema called him to discuss his impending testimony. She was keen that Lal Bahadur should prepare him for what he must say in court. They were a little puzzled when Kuldeep refused to meet her or Lal Bahadur, despite their repeated calls.

'You don't worry,' Lal Bahadur told Seema. 'I'll brief him in the court itself, just before the hearing. He has given a clear statement to the police and is an eyewitness to the abduction. His testimony cannot go wrong.' But when they reached the court complex on the day of the evidence, and began looking for Kuldeep, they discovered that he was sitting with the lawyers of the accused. Lal Bahadur tried to explain to him how he must give his testimony but it was clear that Kuldeep had switched sides.

Sure enough, when the court assembled and he was called upon to testify, he resiled from his previous statement given to the police.

'I don't know anything about this case. I am a contractor at the toll plaza which is being constructed near village Manak Majra on GT Road, I usually go to the toll plaza at 8 a.m. and return at around 6 p.m. every day. On 15 June 2007 at about 4.30 p.m. I was present at the toll plaza, but nothing happened before me on that day,' he told the stunned courtroom.

The public prosecutor M.C. Gaur sprang to his feet and said, 'My Lord, this witness is suppressing the truth as he has resiled from his previous statement made to the police. He should be declared hostile and I may be allowed to cross-examine him.'

'I had been expecting something like this,' Lal Bahadur whispered, grim faced, to his colleague Rajesh. Kuldeep was one of their star witnesses, the only eyewitness to the abduction. Deep down the lawyer felt dejected and wondered how many more witnesses would turn hostile.

Gaur cross-examined Kuldeep, but the latter stuck to his guns and denied everything he had told the police earlier. 'I have seen the statement Ex P1 [exhibit P1]. I have never made such a statement to the police. I never said that a Scorpio along with ten to twelve persons forced a girl and boy to get down from the bus and took them towards Karnal. I also did not say that these persons beat the boy before forcing him into the Scorpio.' Kuldeep also denied recovering or handing over the sports shoe belonging to Manoj, which had fallen off during the scuffle. He denied ever having identified the photographs of Manoj and Babli as those of the abducted boy and girl. He admitted to the court that the signature on the recovery memo of the shoe was his but claimed that it had been obtained by the police on blank paper. He, however, admitted that he was present at the toll plaza as a contractor, but when asked if his denials were due to pressure from the Jat Mahasabha, Kuldeep's answer was an emphatic no.

*

In February 2009, Dr Rajat Pankaj, medical officer posted at the public health centre Jai Jai Wanti in Jind district, deposed. He brought with him the original post-mortem reports conducted by him on the bodies of Manoj and Babli in June 2007. He had been posted as demonstrator in the department of forensic medicines at PGIMS, Rohtak, at that time.

His report read:

> Dead body of unknown female, aged about 25 yrs. It was 160 cms long and was wrapped in a white gunny sack wearing a green kurta torn in places, a white bra, a black salwar torn in places, a yellow metallic ring in the left ring finger, a pair of white metallic pajebs around both feet. The body was emitting a foul smell, maggots of size 5.1 cms were crawling all over the body. Both legs were tied by means of two ropes with a fixed knot. Scalp hair peeled off. All the neck structures were missing. Chest wall hard and shrivelled as also abdominal wall. Body and axillary hair peeled off. Epidermis peeled off. Clusters of maggots present in the genitalia. Fingers of right hand and right foot missing. Ends of long bones fused. Medial ends of clavicle in process of fusion. The uterus was empty.

He had recommended a chemical analysis of the viscera and a diatom test to determine the cause of death.

> On the same day, I also conducted the post mortem on the body of an unknown male aged about 26 yrs. That dead body was about 173 cms long and was wrapped in a white gunny sack wearing a blackish shirt. It was emitting a foul smell, maggots crawling all over it. Scalp hair peeled off except few tufts of black and grey hair in occipital region. Eye balls putrefied and softened. Ears, eyes and lips deformed. Face not identifiable. Finger tips of both hands showed gnawing effect. Penis and scrotum distorted. Rectum protruding . . . That ligature material in the form of a plastic rope that was tied around the neck in two plies, two times by a fixed knot and the lower end of which was tied around both legs, both knee joints with a fixed knot. A reddish ligature mark of width varying from 4 to 5 cms was present all around the neck, 6 cms below the chin. On dissection, the right cornu of hyoid bone was fractured with infiltration of blood in the fracture segments. That in my opinion the cause of death in this case was strangulation by ligature.

He had estimated that the time between death and post-mortem of both bodies was between one to three weeks.

He told the court that since diatoms had not been detected in the forensic examination of the girl, the death had not taken place due to drowning, as was being projected by the defence.

The prosecution seized upon the mutilated penis and scrotum and argued that Manoj had been brutally tortured before being killed. Lal Bahadur was on his feet for most of that hearing but the defence sought to play it down, as being a consequence of putrefaction.

*

The village chaupal at Karoran was swarming with yet another panchayat. For more than a year now, panchayats in the village had become a regular feature and almost all were called to discuss or rule on some issue or the other connected with the Manoj–Babli affair. This time it was bigger than usual and there were some outsiders too. The ones in the know had taken up positions from early morning and white-clad men clustered around gurgling hookahs. Throngs of curious onlookers—male only—added to the crowds. The issue at hand was how to make Seema and Chandrapati withdraw the case against Suresh, Rajinder and others. More urgently, it was to persuade them not to depose in the case as their statements were due to be recorded by the sessions court soon. The two women had so far put up a good fight against the threats and intimidation they had faced from the day Manoj had eloped with Babli and through the months following their brutal murders. Much against the expectation of the khap leaders and despite the support and protection they got from the village, the accused had been arrested and were being tried in the glare of hostile media coverage. 'It was certainly not on. Something had to be done to stop it all.'

With no elderly man left in their family 'to drill sense into the stubborn women', the village leadership decided to bring in men from Chandrapati's native village, Danauda, and also her sister's husband and son from Kori to do the needful. There was a brief discussion in which it was decided that the panchayat would go to Chandrapati's house and then let the relatives do the talking. The throngs shifted to her small house. When the small courtyard became full, people squeezed into the narrow lane outside. Some climbed the rooftops of neighbouring houses to watch and listen.

Chandrapati's brother-in-law was the first to speak.

Addressing the two women, he said, 'What is done is done. The dead can never come back, but you have to live here in this very village. If this case carries on you will have a lifetime of enmity with Babli's powerful family.'

Even before her mother could open her mouth to speak, Seema took off. 'There is already enmity, Mausa, you don't need to bother about how we deal with it. Where were you when we were singled out and shunned by the whole village?'

Chandrapati stood up and adjusted the dupatta on her head. 'Did you stand by me and my children when we were running from one police thana to another to get even an FIR registered? Today you are coming to my door in the company of my oppressors,' she screamed. Mausa was taken aback. He had not expected such belligerence.

Putting on a reasonable voice, he said, 'We understand your anguish. But now you have to think of your two daughters. The only sensible thing is to withdraw your case and go in for a compromise. This is my advice.'

Seema was beside herself with anger. Any talk of compromising with the killers of her brother and sister-in-law made her see red. She turned on her uncle with fury. 'There is no need to give us advice now. We are your relatives, yet our sorrow and hardship mean nothing to you. You are standing and siding with these people who have no relationship with you. Why? For us, you all died during those days when our boy died. When none of you came to condole his death or be with us when we immersed his ashes. We have managed very well without you so far, Mausa, and will manage in future too,' she yelled, and the crowds heard her in rapt silence. Her cousin stepped forward to say something but his father stopped him.

His volume had come down a few decibels. 'Seema, you are like a daughter to me. I am giving you fatherly advice as an elder in the family.'

'Daughter?' she laughed derisively. The hurt and anger at being deserted by these relatives in their hour of need had rankled long and deep. This was the time to vent it. To show that she was not prepared to extend him even the basic courtesies due to an elder. *'Tu chup kar, Mausa!* Just wearing a pugri on your head does not bestow you with sense and wisdom. If you had any sense you would not be siding with these people today,' she raged. The people on the rooftops began murmuring, and her uncle's face turned red.

'Theek hai. You do what you want to do,' he said tersely and walked out of the door. Seema was left shaking. Chandrapati picked up the fodder container and went over to where the buffaloes were tied. Taking the cue, the swarm evaporated with a collective rustle of clothes.

There was no let-up in the pressure on them. Another day it was Rampal Majra who came. He was a former legislator of the INLD, who had represented their assembly constituency of Pai a couple of years earlier. The first time he came, Seema was at Karnal, undergoing her police training. When Chandrapati called to inform her of Rampal's visit and his offer to broker a compromise, Seema's first words were, 'Ma, why did you even let him into the house? You know all these people are coming now only to make us back down. We have to take this fight to its logical conclusion.'

A few days later, the politico made another visit and this time Seema was at home. It was the same old spiel. 'A compromise is the best solution for both sides. You will not gain anything by earning their lifelong enmity,' he cranked on.

Seema then reminded him that whenever there was a death in any family in the constituency, as the local legislator, he had always come to offer his condolences. 'We had not one but two deaths in our family. But you did not think it necessary to visit our house even once to condole with us? You knew that the entire village had shunned us and you joined them in boycotting us. You picked us out for this treatment.'

Pointing towards Manoj's garlanded picture inside, she carried on, her voice trembling, 'This is the same Manoj's house, Rampalji, who had married into his own gotra. We were pariahs for you then. What has changed now that you have deigned to enter our doorway?'

Rampal had been warned that he would have to face hostility from Seema. The girl had emerged stronger and more confident from the crisis and seemed ready to take on more. He ran his fingers though his thick but prematurely greying shock of hair and was wondering how to get out of this situation. As he rose to leave, Seema delivered her last shot: 'You did not come [to us before] because your vote bank is on the other side. They can get you the numbers, but we are nothing for you.' This was not going according to the script the panchayat had outlined for him. The girl packed quite a punch and he realized that he was not equipped to deal with her. 'Think it over, Seema. See what can be done,' he mumbled before hurrying out.

*

The court had fixed 10 August as the day for recording the evidence of Chandrapati and Seema. They could sense the tension building up, as the opposite camp had tried every trick in the book and outside to persuade them not to depose. Seema had finished her training and was given a posting in the police training academy at Madhuban itself. She took a few days off from work to prepare her mother and herself for presenting the all-important evidence and together they took extensive briefings from Lal Bahadur.

He spent hours making Chandrapati mug up the telephone numbers, and some words in English that she would have to pronounce. The illiterate but feisty woman mastered it all.

Just a day before they were to depose, they had a visitor. What he said spooked them. Shamu is known in their locality as the village drunkard and few take his words seriously after dusk and sometimes even during the day. He dropped by their house in the morning to tell them that Manphool and two others were planning a murderous attack on them at the Karoran bus stand the following day, to prevent them from deposing. He had gleaned this information while drinking with them the previous evening, and as soon as his hangover lifted in the morning the good-hearted fellow realized that he must warn the two women about what awaited them. 'Chachi, be careful, they have arranged firearms and told me, *hum unka dhuan utha denge*. They plan to attack you at the bus stand,' he said.

They huddled together in a nervous panic. The simple lunch of dal and rotis which Rekha had made went cold as they debated what to do. Narinder took charge and decided that they should leave the village that very day. At once. 'It's the only way to outwit Manphool. If he is going to wait for us at the bus stand, it won't do for us to be either there or anywhere else in Karoran,' he uttered in a low voice. Chandrapati agreed immediately and suggested that they spend the night at Premchand's house in Kaithal. 'We will be safe there. No one will guess we are there. Seema, you call and tell him we are coming to his house today.' At 6 p.m., the trio discreetly boarded a hurriedly summoned taxi. It helped that their house is close to the main road which encircles the village. It enters from the Pundri end and exits the village on the southern side where the road goes on to Rahra. Vinod directed the taxi driver to take the roundabout Rahra route to Kaithal so that they could avoid passing through the more public village bus stand where there is always a crowd of nosy layabouts.

The ever-helpful Prem welcomed them at Kaithal and it was unanimously decided that they should hire a taxi the next day too to take them to the Karnal court. Travelling in a bus would give them unnecessary visibility and no protection. Seema found that after paying 1500 rupees for the taxi they would have only 600 rupees left for the remainder of the month. 'It's enough to buy some groceries. I'll have to ask Rekha to take an advance from the people who buy milk from us. Thank God the buffalo is giving milk,' she thought, as she counted out the money they would need the next day. But when they reached the court at Karnal, Lal Bahadur told them that the recording of their evidence had been postponed to the next day, the 11th, as the one of the defence lawyers was not present.

Seema spotted Manphool with two others just as they were making their way out of the court. She guessed that they had been waiting for them at the Karoran bus stand and, not seeing them, the assault team had reached the Karnal court. She stopped dead in her tracks and turned to inform Lal Bahadur about their presence. Even as the two confabulated, Chandrapati had begun walking towards the police post in the court complex. 'Come on,' she gestured. 'Let's tell the police. It might help.' By now they had become familiar figures in the Karnal courts and everyone knew of their case. After the initial reluctance to help them, the police attitude had changed a little, but only just. The cops on duty heard them out. One of them advised, 'Behenji, it will be better if you ask the Kaithal police to provide you some more security for tomorrow. Our responsibility is only within the court complex but you will need protection while travelling from your village to the court.'

They headed back to Karoran in the same taxi but took another roundabout route to reach the village. On the way Narinder worked the phones and contacted the SSP at Kaithal. He apprised the police officer of the plot to attack them and was pleasantly surprised when, even before he could ask, the SSP offered to send four security personnel to accompany them to court the next day. The four policemen reached their house shortly after they arrived and, together with the two guards they already had, the six policemen guarded the family the whole night. They hardly slept that night. The tension was killing them. The presence of Manphool at the court had really frightened Seema. 'So what Shamu told us was true! They did intend to physically prevent us from deposing,' she thought, tossing about on her string cot. Outside, a gentle monsoon rain pattered on the courtyard. Further, towards the main entrance of their house, she could hear the buffalo grunt in pleasure as her calf nuzzled her. The policemen had spread themselves around the house and two of them were on the roof. 'God, I hope the deposition takes place tomorrow. I can't afford a taxi for many days,' was her last thought as she closed her eyes.

*

The day broke over dark monsoon clouds. Cool and wet. The grey clouds above and emerald-green fields made a bewitching contrast as they sped towards the court that morning. In anticipation of their deposition, the courtroom was jam-packed. Scores of people from Karoran, many curious lawyers and litigants from other courts thronged the room. Chandrapati deposed first. Every time she spoke, there were murmurs from the onlookers. Sometimes they laughed and wondered how an illiterate woman was uttering English words. Lal Bahadur enjoyed the attention she was getting. He had worked very hard to prepare her for this testimony, made her repeat the telephone numbers, the brand of Manoj's shoe, Pace, and much else. She told the court that the parcel containing the shoe recovered by Kuldeep after the scuffle at the toll plaza was taken into possession by the police, and sealed with seal DB used by the police, as exhibit P2.

During cross-examination by the defence counsel J.S. Jattain, she admitted that she did not know the date, year or month of her marriage, or even the birthday of Manoj or any of her other children. Chandrapati is completely unlettered and that came through in her two-day-long testimony. But she was razor-sharp in tackling the legal landmines the defence had laid for her. Perhaps it was her innate horse sense or the sincerity with which she negotiated the questions that helped her sail through. She was questioned about the telephone number from which Manoj was calling before he reached Pipli. She told the court that it was given to Manoj by his friend Kala on the morning that Manoj appeared with Babli at the Kaithal court complex. The defence also questioned her about her own phone with number 9416573352, which was actually in the name of Jasmer Singh, the son of Dalip Singh, a distant relative of hers from Kultaran village. It had been with Chandrapati for two years and she was paying the bills. Manoj had made all the calls, first from the cell phone with him and later, when the balance finished, from the STD booth at Parakeet tourist complex in Pipli, to this number. There was an attempt by the defence to prove that Chandrapati had filed the FIR against the accused because of a previous enmity between Dalip's family and Gangaraj. It also came out that Dalip, who was the president of the INLD's Kaithal district unit, had helped Seema to get her first job in the Haryana State Industrial Security Force. But when the defence began questioning her about the nuances of a murder case against Dalip's family in which Gangaraj is a witness (to suggest that she had registered the FIR against the accused at the instance of Dalip) she didn't know much. This line of questioning went cold when it became clear that she was unaware of this old issue between Dalip and Gangaraj.

The next day, they tried to bring in another enmity, this time between Narinder and Gangaraj, which the defence wanted to project as the real motive for accusing Gangaraj and others of murder. Narinder had contested the election for sarpanch some years ago, and lost.

'Did he lose against Gangaraj? Is that why your family nurses a grudge against him?' J.S. Jattain wanted to know.

Chandrapati smiled. 'This is so ridiculous. I could laugh,' she said to herself.

Turning to the court, she was categorical. 'Narinder, my nephew, did stand for the sarpanch election and he lost. But he did not lose to Gangaraj. The FIR of kidnapping that Ompati had registered against Seema, Manoj and me was being pursued by these six accused, namely Gangaraj, Rajinder, Suresh and others. As a result, the Rajaund police was harassing us and it is due to that harassment that we developed a grudge against them. Our enmity, however, began only after the murder of Manoj and Babli.'

The defence was banking on her slipping up while submitting her testimony, as she was uneducated. But she gave a clear account of the day when she and Seema were called to Rajaund police station to identify the articles recovered from the bodies of Manoj and Babli. 'HC Rajesh produced a parcel of belongings of an unknown woman. It was unsealed before me and it contained one chappal, one salwar, six bangles and a pair of pajeb which we identified as belonging to Babli. Seema and I had purchased these articles from the market and given to her. The kameez is of green colour and salwar is black.'

She could also clearly recollect what happened on 26 June 2007 when she, along with Narinder, had gone to the toll plaza to meet Kuldeep with the Butana police. She identified the parcel containing a blue-and-white shoe, with white laces, as being the same one recovered from Kuldeep, parcelled and sealed by the police. No ambiguity or hesitance here.

At the end of it, a bewildered Chandrapati wondered why she was asked so many superfluous questions which had little to do with the case. 'Why were they asking about Jasmer and Dalip? It has nothing to do with our matter,' she said to Lal Bahadur. He just smiled at her. 'It happens.' Seema was made to wait outside the courtroom while her mother deposed. The next day it was her turn to testify.

Lal Bahadur sighed with relief once both their depositions concluded. He was occupied with proving the sequence of events—completing the circle, as he called it. He found himself hampered due to the failure of the police to bring in the evidence from the owner of the STD booth at Pipili and their inability to trace the bus and the passengers from which Manoj and Babli were abducted from the toll plaza. His prosecution's entire case was based largely on circumstantial evidence, but it was clinching, despite the gaps. Lal Bahadur's strongest points were the disclosure statements of Mandeep, the driver of the silver-coloured Scorpio, and the other accused, in which they admitted to killing Manoj and Babli. Disclosure statements made by the accused before the police as such are not admissible as evidence in the courts, because Section 26 of the Indian Evidence Act 1872 states that no confession made by any person while he was in the custody of the police officer, unless it was made in the presence of a magistrate, shall be proved as against such a person. But a proviso under Section 27 of the act says that if the information leads to the discovery of a material fact, it could be used to prove the offence against the person who had made the confession.

The police normally use disclosure statements as a take-off point for investigations and to corroborate their own findings. In this case the accused had helped the police to demarcate the area from where the abductions took place, where they were murdered and where the bodies were disposed of. Suresh helped them to recover the bottle of Endosulfan pesticide given to Babli, and Gurdev helped them to recover Manoj's wallet that he had hidden under a brick. It had a photograph of Manoj and Babli in it. Then, from Baru Ram's car, which was recovered from him and subjected to a thorough cleaning, the police had found one button, one ghungroo or anklet bell, a piece of glass bangle and some hair. The forensic science laboratory (FSL) report stated categorically that the button recovered from the car matched the one recovered from the clothes of the dead. A piece of the torn photograph recovered from the Scorpio was found to have been developed from the same negative as the photo recovered with the help of Gurdev. The bell was from Babli's anklet. All this helped the prosecution to connect the accused with the crime. The prosecution had also brought to the attention of the court that after the murder numerous panchayats were convened by the community to ostracize Chandrapati and her family.

*

Additional Sessions Judge Vani Gopal Sharma looked up with a start. The door to the porch was yanked open and her son rushed in, soiled boots and all. It was one of those rare days when both of Vani's children were with her in her small government bungalow in the officers' colony in Karnal.

Her thirteen-year-old son, Raghav, looked forward to these occasions when he could show his elder sister, Niharika, his school projects and games. Vani wished her husband, working as a tax consultant in Chandigarh, had been able to join them this weekend. But when he had called the previous evening to say that he wouldn't be able to make it and that Niharika would, she suppressed her stab of disappointment. 'It's good that Niharika is coming. Stepping into her teens has changed her. I should spend more time with her,' she thought as she had put the phone down after their conversation.

Ever since Vani had qualified for the judicial branch of the Haryana Civil Service in 1993, most of her postings had been in the interior districts of Haryana. She had learned to adjust to a long-distance marriage, where she met her husband mostly on weekends. Niharika had been with her as an infant and when she was in primary school. Now they had decided to put her in a convent school in Chandigarh for the Class X boards, while Raghav stayed with her. Today she was determined not to allow court work, which she sometimes brought home, to eat into the time she wanted to spend with the two children.

She saw Ram Lal, the peon, entering the room with a stack of files in a bag. He put down the bag on the stool near her desk and paused for a bit. '*Sab theek hai, Ram Lal?*' she inquired with a smile. 'Ji madam,' he muttered, still lingering there. Vani waited.

'You know that murder case from Karoran village which is in your court? The girl Seema was slapped two days ago when she had come for the hearing,' he blurted. 'One of the accused slapped her in front of everyone, just as they were being taken out by the police. I thought I should tell you, madam, because you are too busy to take an interest in what happens outside the courtroom. Madam, it created a huge tamasha.' He waited respectfully for a reaction. There was none. Vani was not given to discussing anything connected with her cases with the office staff. And she strictly discouraged gossip of any kind. The news did surprise her and even gave her an inkling of the passions at play in the matter, but she wasn't about to discuss it with Ram Lal. No way.

'*Theek hai. Chai pee ke jaana, Ram Lal.* Ask the cook to make some for you,' she dismissed him.

Vani pulled out the file of the Manoj–Babli case and scanned the testimonies of the witnesses made till then. For her it was a murder trial like any other. Nothing special or extraordinary. She knew very little of the media hype which surrounded it, the politics or the institution of khaps which were influencing every aspect of this matter. Nevertheless, she pondered over what Ram Lal had told her. She spent the better part of the next one hour reading up the Manoj–Babli case file. Niharika stepped in once to check what her mother was so preoccupied with, but seeing her deeply absorbed in a file, the girl tiptoed out of the room.

Vani comes from a social milieu far removed from the world of khap panchayats and clan diktats. Hers is a conservative Marwari family which has made Jalandhar, in Punjab, their home. The third daughter of a retired engineer, Vani had seen gender discrimination at home, between her sisters and her only brother, whom her parents doted on. Very early on she decided that she would be independent, chart out a career, study further and not follow the path of an early marriage as her sisters had done. Vani studied at HMV College in Jalandhar and law at Guru Nanak Dev University, Jalandhar campus. When she married, it was to a Brahmin tax consultant whom she met while doing a diploma course in tax at the Panjab University. Her decision to marry Gopal had created a storm in their family but her mother took the stand that as a qualified lawyer, fighting cases for others, she was capable of taking charge of her own life too. It was hard to oppose an argument like that. For Vani, her housebound, little-educated mother has been an inspiration, for she ensured that her daughter studied as much as she wanted to.

In the fifteen-odd years since she joined the judicial service, Vani had worked her way up to become an additional sessions judge, after having served in Gohana, Kurukshetra, Sirsa, Charkhi Dadri and Jind. She was assigned the Manoj–Babli case in early 2009, and ensured that the strict discipline she enforced in her courtroom was also maintained by the volatile panchayats from Karoran, whose villagers often came to witness the proceedings. Off and on, news reports about this case filtered down to her, but she had never made an attempt to read them herself or follow the shenanigans of the khap panchayats. Vani abided by a self-imposed restriction not to read any news about the cases that were before her. 'It's better to be uninformed. I don't want to know who got hurt and whose children are suffering,' she told herself whenever someone tried to bring up the Manoj–Babli case in her presence. A couple of attempts by friendly lawyers to discuss the case with her alerted her to the possible swirl in this one. More than once she brushed aside the thought and willed herself to concentrate on the arguments before her. For almost a year, recording of the testimonies and hearing the arguments of the case went on. Towards the end of January, Vani found that the time had come for her to pronounce the judgement.

The only preparation she did in those days was to stay up late to read up the case papers. She did that with most of her important judgements. She loved the din of the courts, the disorderly energy of the litigants and, above all, the work that she did in the midst of it all. But when it came to contemplating on arguments made during the day, or crystallizing a decision in her mind, she preferred the quiet of the night. It helped to clarify her thoughts.

*

On 25 March 2010, Vani held all the accused guilty of kidnapping and committing culpable homicide amounting to murder punishable under Section 302 of the IPC. It was a landmark judgement in Haryana, drawing widespread praise and some condemnation too. Never before had a judge convicted perpetrators of an honour crime, and it upset the guardians of Jat social mores and their political supporters, even as those fighting against the custom rejoiced. A petite, soft-spoken woman from Jalandhar had taken on the dreaded khap panchayats. Ironically, she was unaware of the import of her judgement till after it was delivered.

Tractor trolleys full of supporters from Karoran and other villages had descended on the court, to hear its pronouncement. So had the media, print and electronic. As soon as it was made, there was mayhem in the court complex. Outraged by the conviction, the khap members abused the court, the media and anyone else who had a good word to say about the judgement. Media persons pushing to seek reactions from the convicts were heckled and their cameras broken. Matters like this were rarely allowed to reach the courts in Haryana. And here, not only was the case decided in two years flat, it had even led to a conviction! Vani had never seen such bedlam and intimidation in her court. There were threatening gestures against her and an enraged roar all around. It was disconcerting. Things improved when the police escorted her out. That night she broke her own rule and watched the coverage of the day's events avidly on news channels. For the first time Vani became aware of the enormity of her judgement and the forces she had taken on.

The next day's *Times of India* carried this report:

> On Thursday, a large number of policemen were deployed in the court premises to avoid any untoward incident as hundreds of villagers had gathered to hear the verdict. However, no one from Manoj's family was present due to apprehensions of threat to life. The premises erupted into heated arguments as soon as the verdict was given and scribes approached the convicts and their relatives for comment.

Lal Bahadur found himself facing television cameras. 'The verdict will send a clear message to khap leaders—that they don't have a right to take anyone's life,' he said in the initial exhilaration of winning the case. But soon after he gave this statement, he called up the Karnal police and requested for protection to enable him and his team of lawyers to leave the premises safely. An armed escort reached them to Hisar.

The next five days were probably the toughest Vani had ever faced in her professional life. Having held them guilty, she now had to decide the quantum of punishment for the convicted persons. In all her years of being a judge, she had never pronounced the death sentence. As she confided in a friend later: 'I struggled with the decision for days. Till then I had no inkling that this case had such widespread ramifications. But the reaction and crowd which had collected on the 25th surprised me. I weighed the pros and cons, the merits of the case and its procedural details during those five days.' On reading about the ruckus which took place in her court on judgement day, Gopal Sharma hurried to Karnal to be with his wife. He worried for her safety and Vani too was glad to see him at home when she returned from the courts the next day.

In the evening he sat with her in their modest living room, as she had her cup of tea. Vani was quiet and Gopal made no effort to start a conversation. He sensed that Vani would take her time before she told him what was bothering her, but he knew it even before she did. Eventually she put down the teacup and said, 'Did you see the television coverage yesterday?'

'Yes. You seem to have whipped up quite a storm with your judgement. My wife has become a heroine,' he smiled.

His compliment did not evoke a smile in return. Vani was serious. 'I still have to decide on the quantum of punishment: life imprisonment or the death sentence. Gopal, I have never had a reason to award a death sentence to anyone, but this time I feel they deserve it.'

'Then do what you think is right. Why are you so glum?'

'This is not an ordinary murder case. If I give them the death penalty, a lifelong enmity will ensue. I have to live and work here. And then, what about you, Raghav and Niharika?'

They could hear laughter from the children's bedroom. The children were playing a video game and she had already decided not to send Raghav to school the next day. She thought it might be a good idea to send him to Chandigarh for a few days till matters here cooled.

When Gopal spoke, she turned her attention to him once again. 'That's true. But Vani, these are the hazards of your profession. Now that one has come up, it is crunch time for you. Believe in yourself and do what you want to do. You have my full support. We will face the consequences together,' he said, and squeezed her hand reassuringly.

As she was grappling with this dilemma, her helper

reported that some women belonging to the families of the convicts had been seen outside her house that day and had wanted to see her. The lone guard outside the house had shooed them away, but she decided to request the district police to send some more security personnel to prevent unwanted persons from pestering her. The police responded to her call for help and for the next few days she had extra security men around her house.

On 29 March the prosecution led by Lal Bahadur argued that all the accused should be given the death sentence. She heard them out but adjourned the court for the next day. Vani did not sleep that night. Next morning she got up and prayed longer than usual: 'God, please give me the strength to do what I should.' By the time she got up from the prayer mat, she had made up her mind.

Amid the din of the crowded courtroom, it was only her trusted secretary standing close to her who noticed the quiver in Vani's voice as she delivered the death sentence for Suresh, Baru Ram, Rajinder, Satish and Gurdev. Gangaraj was given life imprisonment and a fine of 10,000 rupees. He was also directed to pay a compensation of 1 lakh rupees to Chandrapati. Mandeep was sentenced to seven years imprisonment and a fine of 6000 rupees. The courtroom erupted. Suresh and Gangaraj threatened Vani. 'We will see you,' they shouted in rage. *'Yeh tumne accha nahin kiya,'* said a supporter. The SSP of Karnal was himself present in the court to direct the scores of policemen who had been deputed to maintain order. He stood next to Lal Bahadur and his team. The cops had a tough time getting the lawyers and the convicts out of the court. The district police was apprehensive of violence and the possibility of an attempt to free the convicts. As they were being taken out, television cameras began filming. An enraged supporter took a swipe at the cameramen and was immediately overpowered by the policemen.

'Aise kaise phansi de di? Yeh koi kanoon hai? Dekh lenge hum bhi,' said the infuriated men from Karoran, who were milling around the premises: How could she give a death sentence? What law is this? We'll see her!

This is what Vani's judgement said:

> This court has gone through sleepless nights and tried to place itself in the shoes of the offenders and think as to what might have prompted them to take such a step, but nothing seemed to justify the act of committing such a heinous crime, without even batting an eyelid.
>
> The court is of the considered opinion that the present case does fall within the category of rarest of rare cases, not because murders are not common place, but because such murders shock the collective conscience of society . . . the present case is a classic example and reflects a long-standing tradition of oppression against women. This has to be curbed perhaps by legislation categorizing such honour killings as a separate offence, giving a clear message to the public at large. Whether such kind of action in the name of community and its honour should be allowed in a progressive society, is the question to be asked of society itself.
>
> It is indeed painful that the older generation has already handed down their archaic and shameful inheritance with vengeance to the younger generation as is evident from the age of the accused persons, the youngest of who is 23 years of age the oldest is 51 years old. These are the people who emphatically resist any influence which may create a dent in their supremacy as a caste and superiority of gender against a girl of their own family who dared to choose her

> own spouse. The society as a whole seems to have fed their weak and impressionable psyche which instead of stopping the vice, aggravated it manifold till it reached a frightening scale resulting in the murder of their own kin.

She had word of sympathy for Babli's mother, Ompati.

> I am unable to resist the temptation of making a mention that in the whole scenario, the mother of the victim, Babli has been completely forgotten. She is a woman who must have suffered silently throughout the trial. She did not appear even once during the whole course of the trail either in defence of the accused who are her relatives or to contribute anything on her own. She was never asked by the media as to what she went through while her own daughter was killed by her own relatives and whether she wanted this fate for her daughter or was also a silent spectator as she was killed at the hands of unyielding male family members with whom reasoning, logic and affection take a back seat while the flames of community love, fanned by self styled masters of the society, glossed over by the police, exploited and patronized by the politicians become all-consuming passions which has to be jealously guarded at all cost. Evidently, this extreme action is necessitated by such offenders to protect their structure of property, and the edifice of feudal order which seems to be at the root of this heinous crime.

The negligent and sometimes abetting policemen did not get away either.

> A mention is required to be made about the police officials namely sub inspector Jagbir Singh, HC

> Dharampal, Constable Satbir Singh, lady constable Usha Rani, HC Jai Inder Singh, all of police station Rajaund, who left the victims Manoj and Babli unattended at Pipli bus stand while washing their hands of the responsibility of providing police protection to them while the accused were evidently present in the vicinity of the victims. Their role should be looked into by the Senior Superintendent of Police for taking appropriate action.

As for Kuldeep, the toll plaza contractor who turned hostile, Vani ordered action under Section 344 of the CrPc against him for perjury before the court.

In the following months, HC Jai Inder Singh was dismissed from service while SI Jagbir Singh had to lose two salary increments.

*

Seema heard of the sentences from an excited journalist who called her for a reaction towards noon. After that it was complete bedlam on her cell phone. She was on duty at the Madhuban police academy and journalists of all hues pestered her till late into the night for comments and interviews, until in exasperation she switched off the handset. She had been able to talk to her mother and Rekha for barely two minutes during the day, when they shared their elation at the judgement. In Karoran, no one congratulated them, no sweets were distributed and there were no outward signs of rejoicing in their house. Once again, they were completely alone. Even in their moment of victory.

Part Three

Full Circle

Chapter Eight

Voice of God?

30 March 2009

There was stunned anger in Karoran. The khap panchayat members returned in a foul mood after hearing the judgement at Karnal. From the chaupal where they had gathered to take stock of the situation, furious voices could be heard late into the night. 'How dare she do this to us? Let's go to meet the chief minister and seek a dismissal of this judge. She doesn't know what she is doing,' said somebody.

'It's all the doing of that Janwadi Mahila Samiti and these good-for-nothing policemen. They should be sorted out.'

'And look at our impotent government. Is this what we elected them for? This chief minister has done nothing for our community. Our culture is being threatened because of his inaction.'

'By God, I will not allow these media people to step into the village. Their biased reporting has swayed the court.'

'Five of our men will go to the gallows for no fault of theirs! And they call it justice? Hey Bhagwan! Kalyug is certainly upon us.' And it went on and on . . .

The womenfolk of Karoran knew not to get in the way

when the men were angry. This was one of those days. In hushed tones they carried on their late-evening chores. They strained to catch what was going on in the clusters around the hookahs but did not dare ask their men when they called it a day and stomped home that night.

For many days, the village seethed. The Kaithal police kept a close watch and took the precaution of increasing patrolling around the area. There was palpable tension in the air. The last thing the police wanted was another fracas here.

Chandrapati called up Seema and told her not to come home for a few days. 'The atmosphere here is very tense. Someone might even attack us. If you are seen in the village, it could provoke them. Don't come here this weekend, or until I tell you to.'

'What is this, Ma? I want to come and share this happiness with you all. Here at Madhuban, I can't talk to anyone, no one understands,' said Seema.

'Na, beta, try and understand. We are also not stepping out of the house. The policemen are deployed all over the village and also at home. I'll come to see you soon.' She rung off before Seema could say anything more. The light in the courtyard was kept on the whole night, and for many nights after that. The family could sense that the danger to them had somehow increased. Manifold.

The newspapers of the next few days were full of invectives against the judgement, the judge, Vani, and the JMS activists hurled by various khap leaders. Caste panchayats from across the region condemned the judgement. The matter could not be allowed to rest. Much more had to be done to reassert their clout.

*

The khaps have been an integral part of life in rural Haryana, parts of western Uttar Pradesh and Rajasthan. They exist alongside the elected village panchayats, which are often derisively referred to as dalas (clods of earth). In recent years, the khaps have drawn attention to themselves, mostly adverse, in cases of perceived breach of traditional marriage norms.

The khaps' diktats are usually verbal and observed strictly by the community. (The Banwala khap defended itself, saying no written fatwa had been issued against Manoj and Babli.) For those transgressing traditional marriage norms, the punishment is usually harsh—the ultimate being death. But there are absurd ones, like having to bite a shoe, tying a rakhi on the wrist of a husband or divorcing to marry someone chosen by the khap. Khaps may order social ostracism or order families to leave the village; in one case, even after the birth of a baby, the couple was asked to annul their marriage. (Such diktats clash with the laws of the land and the constitutional provisions that guarantee personal freedoms.)

Ironically, the present khaps, whose very existence is being questioned by neo-liberal activists and an alert judiciary, have a long lineage going back to the reign of the seventh-century ruler Harshvardhan. They served as platforms for redressing grievances, delivering quick and corruption-free justice at village level. It is Harshvardhan who gave them their saffron flag with a deep-red sun in the middle; khap panchayats are said to have coronated the twelve-year-old Harsha in Kannauj. Till the arrival of the British in India, the khap panchayats enjoyed an exalted status. The khaps had members of all communities and were not related to any particular caste or tribe. A collection of khaps was called a sarvkhap, and was unlike the present sarvkhap mahapanchayat, which is invariably dominated by one caste, the Jats.

The sarvkhap panchayat helped Raziya Begum, whose tomb is on the outskirts of Kaithal, when she faced trouble from her rebellious Turkish nobles. She is believed to have gifted 60,000 buffaloes to the sarvkhap in gratitude. In 1287, a sarvkhap panchayat held under Chaudhary Mastpal stood up against the atrocities of Alauddin Khilji and refused to pay the jaziya tax and land revenue and obey his orders on marriage and other social ceremonies.

During the Mughal rule, the khaps gave men and materials to the Marathas against Ahmed Shah Abdali in the third battle of Panipat. They also played a legal role. All suits relating to debts, contracts, adultery, inheritance of property, etc. were decided in these panchayats.

Much changed with British rule in the second half of the nineteenth century, when statutory local self-governing bodies were imposed. Many historians argue that one of the biggest casualties of British rule in India has been the age-old community-based system of cheap and quick legal relief. The decisions of the village panchayats were admitted as the voice of God. The British judicial set-up on the other hand was seen as repressive, arbitrary and expensive. The Haryana state gazetteer records: 'It was neither liked by the people of the country, nor appreciated by the efficient and reasonable British Administrators.' The first Census Commissioner of Punjab (then comprising present-day Punjab, Haryana, Himachal Pradesh and Pakistan Punjab), one Mr Ibbetson, stated his observations on the infirmities of British administration in the Karnal district gazetteer in 1892: 'In many respects our refusal to recognize the village as a responsible unit is a mistake. While we do partly enforce the system of joint responsibility, we wholly deny people the privilege of joint government . . . people especially grumble: andher hone laga (justice is delivered blindly) and secondly they object to our disregard of persons and to our practical denial of all authority to the village elders.' The tampering of institutions like khap panchayats by the British is also seen as one reason this part of the country always remained in ferment during the freedom struggle. It is not without significance that during 1857 the revolt against the British was most vicious and widespread in Haryana. The khaps led and brought the whole area under them. They established 'janata sarkars' which functioned independently for four months, till the British regained control of the region in November of 1857. The failure of the Uprising brought severe punishment for much of what composes present-day Haryana.

Today the institution survives as a parallel, extra-constitutional entity, seeking to preserve its hold over a modern society. Judicial courts have replaced the people's panchayats in the villages. At the village level, the elected panchayats control the development funds and the law does not recognize the khaps. It is only in the domain of social traditions, marriage practices and customs that they still wield some influence. But in this sphere also, the customary laws of marriage, kinship and bhaichara, which they seek to enforce, are becoming increasingly irrelevant in an age of rapid urbanization, industrialization and social mobility, where agrarian communities are not as dependent on each other as before. Elected panchayats have been co-opted sometimes, with the sarpanch or regular panchayat members holding positions in the khaps too.

In 2007, the year in which Manoj and Babli were killed, the activities of khap panchayats were at their peak. Many khap leaders had political aspirations too. Caste superiority and control over their clan provided a ladder to a political career.

This is probably why the members of the khaps bristled at the conviction and sentence passed on the seven accused.

The first decisive step they took was on 13 April. A maha khap panchayat (a grand caste council) comprising some forty khaps of Haryana, Rajasthan and western Uttar Pradesh was convened in Kurukshetra to chalk out their next plan of action. Among the organizers was Mahender Singh Tikait, a powerful farmer leader of North India and head of the Ballian khap, who passed away in 2011. Jyoti Kamal, a young CNN-IBN correspondent, had rushed from Chandigarh, along with a score of other reporters who sensed that the Jat organizations would make a major announcement. Some reporters came from Delhi.

The Jat Dharamsala was swarming with hundreds of men clad in white, which is preferred by men in the villages: white pugris, dhotis, kurtas and pyjamas. The younger men wore sports shoes with their pyjamas; the elderly stuck to rough juttis made of hard buffalo leather. A few green and yellow turbans stood out. Those wearing them were making a statement of their own. They were supporters of the INLD, the Jat-centric political party which has ruled Haryana for several years. Hundreds of young and old, some clutching hookahs, got down from tractor trolleys, Matadors, cars and even buffalo carts. The hookahs were promptly set up in the sunny courtyard and hookah circles got going. In another part of the dharamsala, cauldrons of dal and kadhi were bubbling. Women rolled chapattis and many participants, who had left their homes early, headed straight for the dining area. The mood was grim.

Jyoti hadn't had time for breakfast either, but there was work to be done. He pulled out a packet of biscuits that he had stuffed into his pocket just before leaving and munched on them while his cameraman set up the transmission connections. Other journalists around him were also engaged in setting up their equipment. They took some random shots of the arriving participants and the cooking place. The camera picked up Karoran's sarpanch, Karambir, who looked defiantly into the lens, hands on his hips. Suddenly, someone wrenched their wires out and disrupted the transmission. 'You media people are the real culprits. You are supporting the wrong people, and not giving the correct picture of what is happening in our society,' shouted a squat, well-built young man in Liberty sport shoes. '*Maaro in saalon ko*,' yelled another. Journalists ran helter-skelter. The more intrepid among them moved into nooks and continued filming the fracas. 'We are just doing our work. You can't stop us like this,' yelled Jyoti, but no one was listening to him. For a few minutes there was complete chaos. Someone called out to the policemen who were standing guard outside the dharamsala as a precautionary measure, and they rushed in to quell the melee. After a while, the saner elements among the mahapanchayat told the journalists that, though they would not be allowed inside the hall, they would be briefed about the decisions taken by them after the meeting.

'Sure. But that doesn't mean that we will not collect news through other means,' whispered Kamal, a Karnal-based stringer. He had come to cover the meet for a local news channel and was determined to do a decent story. Who knows, some international news channels might buy footage from him. This was hot stuff.

The journalists learned later that a scuffle had broken out among the caste leaders over who would take credit for the day's meet. Tikait's men began to take charge of the stage but they were stopped by the sarv maha khap organizers like Om Prakash Dhankar and the venerable khap leader Dada Malik Gathwala. Hot words and fisticuffs were exchanged, typical of an argument in these parts, before the meet got under way. Dhankar was fuming. As the head of the mahapanchayat, he was used to giving sound bites to media persons and enjoyed the publicity. The hijacking of the meet by Tikait's men galled him no end, especially because he and his cronies could see the hand of some politicians in the ruckus. He retreated to a corner of the main hall with his supporters and carried on in hushed tones. On the stage Vinod Bala, a recently inducted woman member of the khap panchayat, was speaking. Dhankar murmured, 'Who called these men here? One of them is an accused in a rape case and is on bail. Someone should have stopped him from entering the dharamsala.'

'We will not accept this behaviour. Why are they not letting us talk about the same-village marriages being practised in Sirsa and the Bagri belt? They are Jats too. It makes the community look divided,' said Surinder.

'We'll call another panchayat of our own and discuss these issues there. They are clearly under the influence of the INLD. In Om Prakash Chautala's [INLD president] own village people marry within the village gotras. So how can their men take decisions on what happens in our Deswali belt?' said Dhankar.

'Make sure someone briefs the press on our behalf,' he instructed a crony, and their group moved to take their seats in the hall.

Inside the hall, many angry sentiments were being aired against the judiciary, the law, politicians and activists of the JMS. Gangaraj's supporters from Karoran and elsewhere impressed upon the gathering that they had lost the case because the accused could not hire a good lawyer due to shortage of funds. There was an appeal to the Jat community to contribute generously so that the best of lawyers could be hired to fight the case for them in the high court. A token collection drive began then and there and all Jat households of Haryana were asked to contribute at least ten rupees each for the cause. Someone went around with a white cloth and smelly notes and coins began to pile up on it. White again. Not the sparkling white that khap leaders wore, but a grubby yellowish white with brown mud stains on the side. The cloth bundle bulged with the coins and someone emptied the contents on the stage for everyone to see. 'This,' said the speaker, 'is not enough. Bhaiyo, in the coming days, you will be asked to contribute much more. Please give freely when you are asked to. Remember, it is to protect the honour of our community.'

The presidents of all the major Jat khaps went up to the dais and spoke. The summing-up was left to Satbir Chahal, of Gohana in Sonepat, who headed the Akhil Bhartiya Jat Swabhimaan Sangathan. He gave a rousing speech, and later repeated everything for the benefit of journalists who waited outside.

'We have gathered here to discuss the Manoj–Babli judgement. We feel that it is an attack on our social norms. Such judgements and the Hindu Marriage Act are acting as a protection for young people to indulge in vulgarities like marrying their own sisters, mothers and cousins. We want an immediate amendment in this act, which permits eighteen-year-olds to choose partners against our social traditions. This mahapanchayat has been convened today to send a message to the state government. Make no mistake, this is not an appeal. A society is not made by laws. On the contrary, laws are made for the well-being of society and we don't want such laws which are against our traditions. The government should respond.

'We respect the judiciary and don't want a confrontation with it. But this judgement goes against our social customs and traditions and should be withdrawn. There should be a fresh investigation and retrial of this case. We believe that Manoj and Babli were not killed but they committed suicide as they were overcome by their shameless act. They had been given police protection, so it is not possible for them to be abducted and killed under security.'

There were murmurs of approval. The journalists drew closer. 'This is getting interesting,' thought Jyoti, as he looked around for a suitable spot to do a piece to camera (PTC) for the 5 o'clock news bulletin.

There was the mandatory punch at the JMS too. 'We feel that some mischievous organizations are conspiring to destroy the fabric of our Jat society by encouraging and supporting such couples. They must stop it. As for that Manoj's mother, she is out to grab the land and property of Babli's family through this manouevre. The JMS, the CPI(M) are also encouraging her, but we will not allow them to succeed. The chief minister Mr Hooda and his colleagues should think about making a law that prevents such marriages.'

The journalists did their jobs and went home. In Rohtak, Jagmati frowned when she heard the evening news bulletins in which all the new channels were reporting the mahapanchayat's deliberations. She furiously flipped the channels, not wanting to miss anything that was said. She was perhaps the only one who sensed the full significance of the statements. 'So this is it. Their strategy,' she thought. Jagmati had detected a marked shift in the contours of the 'gotra' debate that evening. She called up Shakuntala in Hisar. 'Did you see the television news, Shakuntala? They are deliberately accusing us of encouraging marriages within a gotra, whereas our stand, as you know, has been to oppose the kangaroo courts such as khap panchayats that are handing out punishments to those they believe are breaking caste taboos. When have we said that boys and girls should marry within the same gotra?'

Shakuntala sighed at the other end of the line. 'You are right, Jagmati. This is vile and baseless propaganda. But remember, we had anticipated something like this. Kamlesh and others were apprehensive of just this kind of attack.'

Jagmati listened, even as her mind raced. Shakuntala continued to speak. 'This is a clever ploy to deflect the attention from their doings. We know what the real matter is. They want to control everything: property rights, norms for women, and more. Their support for not marrying into one's gotra, to avoid genetic inbreeding, obscures their real motives.'

'Hmmm. Do you think we should start a counter-campaign or something? Maybe hold a couple of seminars?'

'No, not immediately. For the moment, let's just wait and see how it plays out. I'm sure there are plenty of astute, educated people out there who will see through this smokescreen,' Shakuntala counselled.

'If I wasn't so angry, I would say they are in a tragic situation. The economy in the villages is flailing, relations between castes are in ferment and the youth culture is so alien. They are trying to cope with all this and regain their waning power using gotra,' Shakuntala interjected.

'We'll have a tough time countering it.' Jagmati's words were to prove prophetic.

*

The last thing Vani wanted was to be in the media glare. Her judgement was being hailed and derided in equal measure and the quiet, mild-mannered woman from Jalandhar began to get intimidated by the attention it was getting in the media. Gopal had returned to Chandigarh but they talked several times during the day on the telephone, sometimes just to hear each other's voice and reassure themselves. 'Gopal, I never realized that it would unleash so much passion. I hope it settles down soon,' she said.

'Have they stepped up your police protection?'

'Yes, two more constables have been posted around the house and I've stopped Raghav from going out to play in the park.'

In Chandigarh, judges of the Punjab and Haryana High Court were also following the developments with interest. Vani was in the courtroom when her secretary came to tell her that Justice Mehtab Singh Gill from the high court would be visiting their court that day. He was the administrative judge for the Karnal district court and in that capacity used to conduct inspections and ensure that discipline was maintained in the court under his jurisdiction. 'Odd!' thought Vani, as she proceeded to gather her papers and drink the remaining water from the glass on her desk. 'No one told us that an inspection is due.' She got up, adjusted her saree and made her way to the chamber of the district and sessions judge where all the judges had been summoned for a meeting with Justice Gill.

She was one of the last to arrive there and quietly slipped into a chair just as the meeting began. Routine matters concerning their court were being discussed and her mind wandered to the news reports she had read that morning. Justice Gill was addressing her. She shook her head and turned to him. 'That was a fine judgement you delivered, Madam Sharma. We are very proud of you,' Justice Gill was saying.

'Thank you, sir.'

'I hope you are not facing any security problem. I have heard that these people threatened you in the court premises. I will personally request the deputy commissioner and the SSP to increase your security cover.' Vani was somewhat startled. She squirmed nervously in her chair, uncomfortable with the attention she was getting. 'Sir, they have given me two more constables,' she said, fiddling with the handbag in her lap.

The newspapers got wind of Justice's Gill's visit and reports began to appear about the threats to Vani and the lack of adequate security for her. One news report said that the Karnal police had been pulled up by the high court. Some days later Vani visited the Punjab and Haryana High Court and again met Justice Gill. The meeting was duly reported and newspapers speculated that she had met the judge to request for a transfer to Panchkula, a satellite town of Chandigarh, falling in Haryana.

'Vani Gopal Sharma Seeks Transfer: Fears for Her Life after Honour Killing Verdict,' said the headline of the *Tribune* of 16 April.

Gopal was on the line. She had had a rough day, and her head ached. 'You didn't tell me that you had sought a transfer to Panchkula?' he came straight to the point.

'I haven't. I don't know how these newspaper reports are appearing,' said Vani as she massaged her temples in a slow, circular motion. The last few days had been tense and every other day there was something or the other about her in the newspapers. Sometimes journalists called her to clarify something they had heard and almost always she preferred not to comment, directing them instead to the sessions judge.

'Vani, do you realize that such news reports are making you look weak and frightened? I don't like to see this, especially when you have such a good record. It might be a good idea to clarify that you have not sought a transfer. That you are not about to run away in fear from the Karnal court.'

'I can't speak to the media directly. It's against the rules. We are required to keep a low profile. If anyone is authorized to speak to reporters it is the sessions judge himself. All I can do is write a letter to him and explain my position. I am also very uncomfortable with all this, Gopal. As if it's I who have committed a crime!' ended Vani.

'Yes, you could do that. It's important to guard against any damage to your reputation and standing because of these baseless reports. I'll call again tomorrow. And do get some sleep. You must put this case behind you as soon as possible and get on with your other work.'

She felt better after talking to Gopal. He had that effect on her.

Since Gopal was in Chandigarh, a transfer to Panchkula would have suited her immensely as the town is almost an extension of the city. It was an unspoken wish of hers, and the high court's administrative department was aware that she would welcome a transfer to Panchkula. Vani also knew that at a time like this her superiors would not be able to refuse her a transfer. She had a valid reason. A lesser person would have seized the opportunity to get a posting of her choice, but Vani, as many had already realized, is made differently.

The next day she wrote a letter to her boss, the district and sessions judge of Karnal, informing him that she had not sought a transfer to Panchkula or anywhere else. 'I own responsibility for my judgement and do not want a transfer from the Karnal court,' she had written.

Curiously, no newspaper reported this development and Vani continued to function normally at the Karnal district court for the next one year. During this period khap panchayats circulated defamatory pamphlets against her. 'This woman judge, Vani Gopal Sharma is part of the conspiracy hatched by the National Women's Commission and some antisocial organizations to defame khaps. She has convicted Gangaraj for the death of Manoj and Babli, describing him as a khap member, whereas he is actually a distantly related grandfather of Babli,' read one of them.

*

The sun is a fiery orb in the month of May in Haryana. Hot winds from Rajasthan sear the landscape to a burnt yellow. Fields are pockmarked with wheat stubble left after harvesting, and the trees, which just a month back were dressed in the fresh green plumage of spring, are coated with summer dust. It's a busy time of the year because the fields have to be prepared for the next crop, and this demands abundant irrigation. Politicians have learned over the years that it's not the best time to hold political rallies. The summer of 2010 proved to be the exception, as there was a flurry of well-attended khap mahapanchayats that were held every other day in one or the other district. They were all convened to discuss the impact of the Karnal judgement and chart the future course of action.

Almost all of them were held in the Deswali belt of the state comprising the districts of Rohtak, Sonepat, Jind, Jhajjar and parts of Hisar and Kaithal. It is the centre of Jat power in Haryana. The Deswali Jats were feeling heady because of their newly acquired clout, as for the first time they had a chief minister (Bhupinder Singh Hooda) from their area.

Incest taboos in the Deswali belt are spread over a wide social canvas. Not only is it forbidden to marry someone from the same gotra or lineage but also from within the village, even if the person is from another gotra, on the grounds that somewhere in the forgotten past they might have a common ancestry. It is also forbidden to marry anyone from neighbouring villages with whom your clan has a bhaichara pact. With rapid urbanization and greater social mobility, and more people leaving the village for work, as much as a fourth of the men remain unmarried because of these traditional laws.

Some of the Deswali traditions do not apply to the Bagri Jats in Haryana, who have somewhat different norms for marriage and kinship. The Bagri Jat belt stretches across the south-western districts of Sirsa, Fatehabad, Bhiwani and parts of Hisar and Kaithal. They are migrants from Rajasthan who settled in these areas over the centuries. The settlers brought with them a variety of clans (gotras), which is why Jat villages in the Bagri belt are known to have even up to forty gotras. The Deswali belt on the other hand rarely has more than five or six gotras in a village. If the Deswali incest taboos were observed in the Bagri belt, it would virtually be impossible for young men and women to find matches. This is why marriages within gotras found in one village are common here. The most significant example is that of Chautala village, the native place of the INLD supremo and former chief minister Om Prakash Chautala. It is common knowledge in Haryana that scores of marriages in Chautala and nearby villages have taken place within gotras from the same village. Not an eyebrow has ever been raised.

Interestingly, the institution of khap panchayats, which are found all over the Deswali belt and even in Jat areas of Uttar Pradesh, Rajasthan and Uttarakhand, is also not so common in Bagri Haryana. Where they do exist, their concerns are more with resolving long-standing enmities between families, matters of landed property, sharing of irrigation water or residential boundaries, than with incest taboos.

So when Om Prakash Chautala became one of the first politicians to publicly support the stand of the Jat Mahasabha and other khap panchayats seeking an amendment to the Hindu Marriage Act, 1955, banning marriages within the same gotra, it was met with some cynicism. 'Yet another politician chumming up to the Jat khaps for political dividends,' said many. He followed it up by submitting a memorandum to the then home minister,

P. Chidambaram, saying his party would support the government if it brought in such a bill.

'There is a lot of discussion in the media about khap panchayats. Our party, the INLD, was the first to support it, as marrying within the same lineage is not right scientifically and medically also. This [marriage within same gotra] and within the bhaichara villages [which share a brotherhood pact] is not in sync with Indian culture,' Chautala told media persons in Delhi.

It was his elder brother, the maverick Pratap Singh Chautala, who spoke up for the Bagri Jats. Raman Mohan, the *Tribune* newspaper's Hisar correspondent, reported the elder Chautala as saying, 'Under the circumstances, any ban on intra-gotra marriages will create serious social problems for the Bagri belt which could ultimately leave the Jats divided.' He appealed to Deswali Jats to think progressively and adopt the marital practices of the Bagris, saying, 'There has not been a single intra-gotra marriage among Bagris. But insistence on bhaichara among the same, adjoining or contiguous villages is impractical and undesirable. Bhaichara and gotra issues should not be confused to the detriment of society.' Explaining the intricacies of their traditions, he was quoted as saying that, earlier, the Bagri Jats avoided four gotras, their own, that of the mother and the gotra to which the maternal and paternal grandmothers belonged. However, in doing so, they found that they were unable to find matches for their children. So, over the decades, they limited the ban to just two gotras, their own (bloodline) and that of the mother (milkline). 'We now marry our children into the gotra of their paternal and maternal grandmothers provided none of the two families hail from the ancestral villages of the grandmothers,' he said.

In the charged atmosphere that prevailed among the

hardliners of the Deswali Jats, however, any attempt at a rational discussion would fall flat. Every khap wanted to have its say in the matter, put in its own word about 'the injustice done to those sentenced to death by the Karnal court' and thump their back for having done their bit to uphold community honour. Several ambitious khap leaders saw in the issue an opportunity to further their political careers. Fights for supremacy, similar to the tussle that took place at Kurukshetra, became common at most mahapanchayats, and eventually the newspapers grew weary of reporting the infighting, of which there was plenty that summer.

Though the Congress was in power in Haryana at that time, and the party's stand at the national level has been critical of honour killings, in the state, the government and its leaders brazenly soft-pedalled the issue. Some like Naveen Jindal, the Lok Sabha MP from Kurukshetra, publicly supported the khaps. There are many who say that he really did not have a choice because they forced him to.

Jindal came on the radar of the khaps on 2 May, at Pai in Kurukshetra district, where yet another mega mahapanchayat was held. Pai is just six kilometres from Karoran. The aim was to turn the heat on the state's politicians and get them to do something concrete. One of the resolutions passed that day was to put the elected representatives of the state on one month's notice to support their demand for an amendment to the Hindu Marriage Act. They also threatened to gherao Naveen Jindal's residence in Kaithal if he did not do so.

Watching the proceedings from his perch near the boundary wall was Om Prakash Dhankar. 'What are they trying to do?' he thought to himself. 'This will not yield any dividends.' He sprang to his feet and in a loud voice declared, 'Bhai, we are not in agreement with this resolution.

Jindal is from the Bania caste which is in a minority in Haryana. He has no voice in matters which concern the Jat community. We should instead be conducting gheraos of Jat leaders like Om Prakash Chautala or the chief minister Bhupinder Singh Hooda.' But Dhankar was outnumbered and the resolution was carried. The following Monday, a group of some hundred men reached Jindal's residence-cum-office in Kaithal.

Jindal met them and heard them out. He then gave them a letter, in which he not only declared his support for their cause, but praised khap panchayats for rendering yeoman service to society, by resolving people's problems even before modern legal systems came into existence. Acknowledging the existence of these panchayats since the time of great rulers like Ashoka and Harshvardhan, Jindal said that these panchayats had always given a 'new direction' to the society. The MP assured the panchayat delegates that he supported their demand and regretted that he could not attend their mahapanchayat. 'I and my family have always respected the society's traditions, customs, beliefs and culture,' Jindal said in his letter, extending full support to the khaps within the ambit of the law of the land. And the rider, 'Please also fight evils like female feticide and dowry.' He rounded it off by telling them that he would seek their guidance from time to time in future.

Naveen's 'khap'-friendly volte-face created a furore in the national media and became the subject of many a prime-time talk show. Newspapers and news channels gleefully dissected his support for the khaps. As a young, foreign-educated MP, the scion of a leading business family, a regular at page-3 parties and an aviator to boot, he was seen as the least likely person to be supporting such archaic institutions, which were receiving much criticism from liberals and modernists. In Delhi, an embarrassed Congress party distanced itself from Jindal's statement. Party spokesman Abhishek Manu Singhvi told reporters that it was the personal view of the MP and that the party does not support any organization which violates the rule of law.

'Individual persons or MPs may have their own opinion. That does not mean there is a change in the stance of the Congress. If customary laws based on customs and traditions violate the rule of law or engage in violence and killing in the name of honour, then the Congress is opposed to it.'

Jindal clarified that day itself and several times after that that, as the elected representative of that area, it is his duty to apprise his party and the government about the sentiments of the people. 'I have done just that,' he told the talk show hosts on national television. 'This is a serious issue and different people have different ways of looking at it. We have to find a solution for this problem within the ambit of the law. We cannot do that by shying away from addressing it,' he clarified. But the damage was done and liberals in Delhi brought out their knives. In Jatland though, the political dividends were immense as Jindal emerged as their favourite non-Jat leader. It was a privilege held for several decades by the late Bhajan Lal, who was thrice chief minister of Haryana.

Chapter Nine

'Nothing Ever Remains the Same'

Jagmati carefully pulled out from her bag the newspaper cuttings she had made the previous evening. She put them in a faded folder which held other clippings relating to the Manoj–Babli case, and pushed it into the bottom drawer of their shabby office table. She made a mental note to request Savita to collect clippings of the next week's developments on the khaps' front, as she herself would be busy with an upcoming seminar.

The JMS works on a shoestring budget where the activists double up as office help and do the filing and paperwork themselves in their spare time. 'We possess all the records of our activities and the cases that we track, but find it hard to locate them at the right time,' Jagmati says ruefully whenever she is unable to find documentation for something she has just discussed. Researchers, journalists and the odd documentary maker working on honour killings in Haryana invariably find their way to her office in search of material. For the past few months filing and documentation in the JMS had suffered because Jagmati herself had been occupied with an exciting new job.

In her younger days, Jagmati was known for her prowess in the games field. She played volleyball so well that she made it to the national team and represented the country in several international competitions. This paved the way for her career as an instructor in physical training and soon she joined the department of physical education in Maharishi Dayanand University (MDU) as a professor. Athletic, well built and articulate, she has retained her maiden surname of Sangwan after marriage. 'I am what I am because of my parents. In the world of sports too, everyone knows me as Jagmati Sangwan. Why should I shed that name?' she tells her friends and colleagues. Her heart has always been in gender issues and few outside Rohtak know of her job in MDU. It is as the president of the Haryana unit of the JMS that she is better known. Her activities earn her accolades as well as brickbats, both of which she takes in her stride cheerfully.

In 2010, when the university established a department of women studies, Jagmati was the first choice as its founder-director. She was delighted. Here at last she had an opportunity to work in a field where she could make a difference. She was just three months into her new job when the Karnal court's judgement on the Manoj–Babli case came. It changed her life.

The JMS was jubilant at the judgement and felt vindicated that their efforts at raising awareness about honour killings and extending support to affected families like that of Chandrapati had begun to show results. Most times in such cases the families themselves shied away from taking a stand and the activists would feel helpless. But Seema and Chandrapati had never once hesitated and the JMS ladies never ceased to marvel at their determination. Within a month, however, they realized that they had opened themselves up to the ire of the mighty khaps like never before. The organization, and Jagmati herself, was targeted in the series of mahapanchayats organized across Haryana following the judgement, and held responsible for 'inciting our youngsters to marry their own sisters and brothers, by encouraging marriages within a single gotra'.

'This is really getting too much. We can't just sit back and let them get away with such baseless accusations,' said Jagmati flinging her handbag crossly on the couch and reaching for the television remote to tune in to the live proceedings of yet another khap meeting being telecast by a local news channel. 'Look at this. We are being branded as destroyers of the Jat social fabric. Enemies of tradition and culture. Who will not fall for this propaganda?' she hissed. Her husband, Inderjeet, looked up from the newspaper he was reading and nodded. He knew what she meant but waited for her fury to subside. He understood his wife quite well. Despite her firebrand image outside, she generally did what he suggested in his quiet, unassuming manner.

'You could try contradicting them by writing articles in major newspapers. Pick holes in their argument and justify your stand,' said Inderjeet. 'I'll help you, if you like,' he added.

Jagmati jumped into the fray, adding her bit to the cacophony of opinions being carried in the various newspapers. In *The Hindu* of 8 May, she wrote:

> Most of the khap diktats are against couples who are not from the same gotra. In fact, not more than one case of honour killing has taken place of a couple from the same gotra. By creating an impression that all marriages of choice between young couples are incestuous, what the Khaps are actually opposing is the right to choose a marriage partner. Among the several instances of Khaps issuing 'fatwas' in Jaundi, Asanda, Dilarana, Singhwal, Hardaudi, Meham Kheri and other villages, not a single one was an intra

> gotra marriage yet the married couples were declared as siblings and the families made to suffer social boycotts and excommunication from their villages.

She gave the example of the gotra row which led to the death of Vedpal Moun in Singhwal village in 2009.

> He was brutally beaten to death last year when he tried to secure his wife who was confined by her parents at Singhwal village in Jind district. He was escorted by a police party and a warrant officer of the high court. Ved Pal had married neither within his gotra nor within the same village. In his case the khap had invoked another absurd code that the couple had violated the custom of not marrying in the neighbouring or 'bhaichara' villages. A khap congregation held in March 2009 publicly pronounced a death sentence for Vedpal and it succeeded in executing it in June. As couples are selectively targeted, it is clear that the real motive is to control women's sexuality and to ensure that property remains within the patriarchal caste domain (mainly Jats in Haryana).

She followed it up with another article in the *Times of India*. By then the backlash had begun.

It began with an article by a Haryana-based journalist, Pawan Kumar Bansal, on a web portal, Merinews.com, in which he put up a reasoned argument in defence of the khaps and advocated an amendment to the Hindu Marriage Act. About Jagmati, he wrote, 'Same gotra marriage legal, court had ruled 65 years ago by Bombay High Court, says Jagmati Sangwan in a leading English newspaper of the country.'

She had offered a clarification, saying that the remarks

had been wrongly attributed to her because her picture was printed along with another article in the *Times of India*. The article written by her was actually in the inside pages. Disregarding this response, within hours abusive comments against her began piling up.

'Look at this one,' she fumed while reading the comments on her office computer to Savita who had dropped by. 'This is clearly a planned initiative, because if you notice, hardly anyone is debating the points raised in the article; they are busy hitting out at me.'

She clenched her teeth and began reading: 'I have attended your lecture at KU recently. I have not seen such a shameless and attention-seeking lady in my life. What are you promoting for your own gain? The fact is that you are neither a Jat nor a social person. You have no social understanding. Would you let your son and daughter sleep with each other in the name of modernity?' One Ramesh had posted this on 25 May.

'You should issue a rejoinder to this website to check abusive comments like this, and after that please ignore such comments. If we begin paying attention to mala fide talk like this, we'll never get any work done,' Savita instructed.

Jagmati hadn't told her everything. Trouble was brewing for her on another front. Something more serious than the abusive tirade. She thought she would discuss it with Inderjeet before telling her JMS colleagues.

In the last few days, she had learned of complaints being sent to the MDU vice chancellor, Dr R.P. Hooda, painting her as a rabid antisocial activist, who was using her position in the women studies department to further an agenda. The Jat intellectuals who attacked her extended her the courtesy of sending a copy of their emails to Dr Hooda.

Dr J.K. Gehlawat, a former professor of the Indian Institute of Technology (IIT) Kanpur, had written:

> I am a former Professor of IIT Kanpur. These days I am doing social engineering. Your esteemed father-in-law was my friend. He was an active member at Delhi State Centre of Institutions of Engineers (India). We used to meet at the Engineers Bhawan, ITO, New Delhi, frequently when he talked very highly of you.
>
> I take this opportunity to add to the information Col M.S. Dahiya and Shri Diwan Singh have given to you about the objectionable and irresponsible activities of your Teacher Smt. Jagmati Sangwan. I had learnt about her anti-Khap activities. I listened to her talking nonsense at the studio of PTC News Channel, Mohali (Punjab), on 12 February 2010. Generally, she moves with some disgruntled school teachers who talk ill about Khap Panchayats without any substance. My report on the said Mohali TV recordings is sent as attachment (page 17 of March 2010 issue of Jat Jyoti) for your information and records. Kindly advise Smt. Jagmati Sangwan to do her given academic work than play in the hands of Media for cheap popularity.

She also received two emails from one Col (retd) M.S. Dahiya, who after retirement had immersed himself in studying khap panchyats and the thirty-six biradari social systems. The first one had warned her that he would be writing to the VC about her misdeeds.

His formal complaint to the vice chancellor says:

> I wish to bring to your notice the activities of one of your faculty member (Ms Jagmati Sangwan) who flaunting the tag of your university & heading some women study center, is spreading a lot of mis-information about our people & their centuries old

social system, in fact their way of life & demanding a ban on them. While i do not say that it is 100% trash, but definitely not based on any authenticated research (as expected from any one who claims association with a university) & is dominated by her personal observations /biases . . . I wish to clarify from your good self whether this lady prof & a employee of the MDU has the NECESSARY PERMOSSION from the university & she is a trained professor in the subject & the views expressed by her have the stamp of the MDU? Why I am asking is that she is not mending her ways & persuing a smear campaign demanding a ban on a people & thus disturbing the peace in the society. It is also alleged that she is running a NGO & is doing this on behalf of the donor agency .what ever be the truth, may i request you to look into the matter & confirm or negate my apprehensions before it is too late. After all this smear campaign is being run by Taxpayer money & incidentally the same people against whom it is directed. I sincerely beg your pardon for the inconvenience.

Regards& best wishes

Col MS Dahiya

Jagmati fumed, and waited for Dr Hooda to react. It happened a few days later when she was summoned to his office where, to her consternation, she found that her deputy director was also present.

Dr Hooda is a specialist in economics and has held administrative positions in reputed educational institutions for long years. He had personally brought Jagmati to head the newly created women studies department because of her work in the field of gender issues. 'Jagmatiji, as you are aware, I am delighted to have you heading this department. You are my first choice for this position,' he began.

She knew that she hadn't been called for a pep talk, so she smiled and waited. 'You know there is this controversy about khaps and intra-gotra marriages in Haryana. Your department has also been organizing events to discuss these issues. I wanted to know your views on the role and functioning of khaps.'

Jagmati hesitated for a moment, before replying: 'Sir, my view cannot be different from the law of the land. It is the same as that which is enshrined in the Constitution. I don't support murder and annulment of legal marriages between adult boys and girls, to protect the honour of a particular caste or community. No tradition or customary law should be allowed to violate laws which have been framed under the Constitution.'

'I agree with you . . . It is the actions of a handful of uneducated and backward people who are preventing the community from progressing.'

'Yes, sir.'

'While we are appreciative of the work you are doing in the department, your activities in your NGO are causing some problem. University employees should exercise restraint. After all we are dealing with impressionable students and we should be conscious of the impact our actions can have on them.'

'Yes, sir.'

'That will be all. Good day, Madam Jagmati.'

She walked calmly out of the office, down the grimy corridors, curling up her nose while passing the stinking students' toilet on the ground floor and slowly climbed up the stairs to reach her department on the second floor. It wasn't the vice chancellor's words that hurt her as much as the fact that he had chosen to deliver his warning in front of her junior, the deputy director. 'How mortifying! I wonder if he did it deliberately.'

Jagmati saw herself first as an activist and then as the head of her department. The JMS is her passion, pride and ideology. She was certain that there could be no compromise on the stand that her organization took on contentious issues, particularly now that they had begun to get some success.

*

Darshan was finding it hard to concentrate on the blood test plate he was preparing from a patient's sample. Is it for testing haemoglobin or a routine TLC count? He stopped to check the doctor's slip attached to his laboratory's form. Both. Okay, haemoglobin first. He shook the sample vigorously, put a few drops in a narrow enclosed tube, dribbled a couple of chemical solutions into it and placed it in the stand. 'Should not take more than five minutes,' he thought to himself as he picked up a strip of glass again to smear it with the remaining sample. His mind went back to his father's words that morning. 'Don't do anything rash. You might be working in Kaithal but we have to live in this village. You have your whole life ahead of you to contest elections,' the old man had said, just as he was rushing out to catch a bus which brought him to his laboratory in Kaithal. Another patient walked in and he got busy taking a fasting sample from the man's vein. By the time he broke for lunch, Darshan had collected over twenty samples, was irritable and wanted to go home and finish the morning's conversation.

He badly wanted to contest the panchayat elections due to be held in June in their district and had been silently preparing himself for it for a couple of years now. He always felt that if he had to make a difference in his village, make it a better place to live in, he would have to be the sarpanch one day to steer things in the direction that he wanted.

Everyone in Karoran knows Darshan as the hot-headed rebel of their village. A laboratory technician in a private laboratory in Kaithal, he is among the few boys from the village who went out to study and, on their return, began to look at their age-old traditions with new eyes, to question the village leadership structure in which the elected panchayat is usually subservient to the khap panchayat. It is his wont to oppose the latter at every given opportunity, because, as he tells his friends, 'They are never on the side of development and progress. If it wasn't for their double standards and social hypocrisy, our village would be better off.' He opposed the khap panchayat boycott of Manoj's family for registering an FIR against Babli's relatives, and he was among the group of men who went to Chandrapati's house to break the social boycott by having tea at her home. Two years ago he had led a dharna in protest against the electricity department's failure to provide regular power supply to their village. Karoran has a 33 KVA substation built on some two hectares of land donated by the village panchayat. The panchayat had donated the land on the assumption that at least their village would get electricity round the clock. That never happened, and they continued to get electricity for six-odd hours a day, like the other villages. Darshan and his band of young supporters had begun to ask questions of the power department and, getting no response, they began a protest demonstration.

'Since the substation is built on our land, our village should get uninterrupted power supply or else the department should compensate our panchayat for this land so that the money can be used for other development activities in the village,' he had said, addressing the protesters gathered on a grassy patch in front of the substation. It resulted in the department registering an FIR against Darshan. But the ultimate put-down for him was when the village panchayat did not support his initiative. He was told to put an end to the dharna as it was 'bringing a bad name to the village'. Darshan swore that when panchayat elections came next time around, he would stand for sarpanch.

'We have to rid ourselves of these good-for-nothing drunks, masquerading as leaders. Look at the filth in the village. There are no proper street lights, and not even one of our nine ponds is pucca. And have you noticed that the air surrounding the village smells like a sewage drain?' he grumbled to his friend Krishan one day. Krishan is employed in the public health department on duty in the village itself. They had gone over these problems ad nauseam and so far it was just a lot of hot air generated among his circle of friends. But Darshan was waiting. In the summer of 2010, panchayat elections began to be held in phases in Haryana. In Kaithal district, polling was scheduled for June. He was one of the first to fill the nomination form, and six other men from Karoran also threw their hats into the ring. A few days later all of them withdrew.

The Banwala gotra khap had decreed that they would boycott panchayat elections in all their villages in protest against the Manoj–Babli judgement. A carload of members of the khap panchayat came to Karoran from Singhwal in Jind and the Karoran panchayat convened a hurried meeting in the village chaupal to receive them. The men from Singhwal had come with the message from Pavanjit Banwala (then head of their khap) that all the Banwala villages were boycotting the elections and that the Karoran members should persuade the people who had filed nomination forms from their village to withdraw them.

On hearing the commotion in the chaupal, Krishan went to see what was happening. Like Darshan, he is among the young and restless persons who are critical of the khaps and has been trying to get the elected panchayat to step up development in the village. When he heard about the proposed boycott, Krishan saw red. 'Tau, this boycott is anti-development. If we have no panchayat, all the development work in the village will come to a standstill. Already, we've got a bad name in the media,' he addressed the dominant cluster sitting in the centre of the aasan.

'Arre, you youngsters don't realize that it's important for the whole village to put up a united face. These development works take their own time. Where is the hurry?' said Satpal tau, one of the oldest men in the village. Others joined in. 'Yes, yes. Our village should be one in such matters. See how our fellow Banwalas are supporting us? It is a matter of honour for us.'

Krishan could see that he was outnumbered and some of those on whom he had counted for support had averted their eyes. But he wasn't going to back down without making his point. 'In that case why doesn't the khap persuade all the khaps of Haryana to boycott the elections? They have supported us throughout this issue and can do so even now. We all know that money is being collected from many districts and different khaps to fight the case against our village men. They can just as well join our boycott too.'

A couple of men got up from the string cot and approached him. 'Krishan, you don't know what you are talking about. Go home and leave these decisions to us. We'll listen to you next time.' He left the aasan in disgust just as some of the active members began apportioning to themselves the individual responsibility of making the candidates withdraw their forms.

When Darshan returned from work in the evening, he found two of the khap-type seniors in serious discussion with his father. 'What could it be?' he wondered, as he hurried to wash his hands at the handpump in their courtyard, before entering the baithak where they were sitting.

'Darshan beta, you will have to withdraw your nomination form for election. As you know, the Karnal court has inflicted an injustice on our khap and we have decided to boycott these elections,' said one of them. Darshan knew him vaguely as Mohar Singh from Billa patti. Mohar Singh puffed on the hookah proffered by Darshan's father but did not meet Darshan's eye. Darshan was furious. His dream of becoming a sarpanch was ending even before it had begun. But it wouldn't do to lose his temper before these men. 'Use your tact, Darshan,' he told himself, and took a deep breath.

'Tau, what you are saying is fine. The traditions of our society are as dear to us as to you, but as you know, if we don't have an elected panchayat the entire village will suffer in so many ways. The government will simply ignore us and divert our share of development funds to some other village. It will be our loss. Will the khap compensate us in any way?' he reasoned.

Mohar Singh coughed and cleared his throat. 'Beta, the boycott is only for this time. Whenever panchayat elections are held again, we'll elect one for our village. But we cannot defy the Banwala khap, which is doing so much for our cause.'

Darshan thought for a moment and opened his mouth to speak, but his father waved a silencing hand at him. 'You let me handle this.' And turning to Mohar Singh, he said, 'These young boys don't understand the value of community honour. I take the responsibility of making him withdraw, you don't worry. Ours is a respected family of this village. We will never compromise on its prestige.' This morning, just before he left for work, his father had reminded him about the khap decision. He felt a flush of anger but didn't reply. His father had retired as a schoolteacher from Karoran senior secondary school and Darshan knew that, with a lifetime spent in the village, the patriarch was steeped in the old ethos. He did not even look at the parathas and lassi laid out by his mother, and when he closed the courtyard door to exit, he could sense the tension in the air he left behind. It bothered him the whole day as he mulled over the options available to him, if he did not withdraw. But by the time he put away his syringes at the end of the day, Darshan had made up his mind. He would have to put his aspirations on hold. He didn't want to go against his grain and defy his father. The next day, he and the others withdrew their forms and Karoran's boycott was registered.

Once again Darshan and Krishan's group of literate, job-holding men had failed to change the village mindset, because they are a minority. Most of them had gone out of Karoran to study in Delhi or Gurgaon, and had returned with a wider world view which made them impatient, even contemptuous, of the regressive hold of the khap on the village. '*Kya karen, bhai?* These khapis will never relinquish control,' said Darshan, running his fingers through his hair. They had gathered near the pump house to lick their wounds. A warm wind from the west had blown relentlessly during the day, but now it was still. The evening cool was beginning to creep up from the watered fields, as they squatted in the dirt.

Krishan spat on the ground. 'It's not just our khap, they are the same all over Haryana. Hypocrites all. They bash up their mothers and sisters at home and claim to be the voice of God in the chaupals. Have they ever raised a voice against female feticide? Or the thousands of tribal women from Bengal, Assam and elsewhere, who are being bought to cohabit with our men?'

'I would reckon there are about thirty such women in Karoran alone. What do you say?' said Darshan thoughtfully.

'More, I would say. With a horribly skewed female sex ratio, there aren't enough girls for our men to marry and these people are occupied with gotra issues which impose more restrictions on marriages. Has there ever been a panchayat to punish someone who has killed his daughter in the womb? No. Never one to punish those bringing brides from outside, either. How come that is acceptable?'

'It's such a warped logic! They will never change, even if the whole Jat community goes to the dogs. And why should they? They get their chaudhar, clout, from such diktats. Bas, eat and drink at others' expense. Buy a woman from outside and muzzle people like us who question them. Shameful!'

Krishan had begun to doodle in the mud with a twig. Concentric circles, then triangles. 'We threaten their fiefdom. Who knows tomorrow there might be a diktat against us too,' and he drew a line right across his art. 'Our elders will order us into silence to uphold the family's honour. The end. That will be it.'

Darshan said nothing. Krishan's prophecy hung in the air. He crushed the twig in his hand into tiny bits. Threw the pieces in the air and watched them struggle against the breeze before they fell. 'I have noticed that most of these khapis privately accept that the khap should raise the issue of female feticide and resultant shortage of girls. They seem quite reasonable when you talk to them individually. But as soon as they enter the aasan it is as if someone has changed their internal chips or hypnotized them. They toe the same old line. I feel impotent at such times. What is the use of getting an education and broadening our minds when we are unable to do anything?'

Darshan suddenly smiled. 'C'mon, stop being so melodramatic. Nothing ever remains the same. It will change some day.'

'Let's see . . . Chal, let's have tea and samosas at the shop. It'll brighten my mood.'

Chapter Ten

'Things Are Not the Same Now'

Chandrapati was incensed. When she heard about the boycott of panchayat elections by the Banwala khap a few months earlier, she had swallowed the insult. The jabs from the khap had stopped hurting now. But here was the district administration preparing to hold zila parishad elections and once again the Banwala khap had decided to boycott. Not only that, some khap members were going to be deployed around the polling booth to prevent villagers from casting their votes. Narinder had brought them this news which he had picked up from Darshan and Krishan at the bus stop. 'Taayi, they are doing it again. Boycotting the zila parishad elections too! Will it change anything?'

Chandrapati moved the firewood in the hearth and looked up, her eyes reddened by the smoke. The family hadn't seen her in a temper for months now, so no one noticed how angry she was.

Panchayat and zila parishad elections are held in one go in Haryana although polling is done in two phases. A zila parishad is a government body at the district level, which looks after the rural administration. In addition to the elected members, it also has chairmen of panchayat samitis as its members. The state election machinery began preparations for these elections a few weeks after the panchayat polls. Polling booths were being set up in major villages of the district, and since Karoran is one of the bigger villages in Kaithal, officials had arrived to set up a booth here.

Until the deaths of Manoj and Babli, Chandrapati had taken very little interest in village politics, but grappling with the shenanigans of panchayats, traditional and otherwise, in the last two years had taught her a few things. She knew, for instance, that despite the domination of a clique who occupied positions of importance in both the khap and the elected panchayats, there was a young and restless constituency out there, frustrated with their inability to change things. Darshan represented this section and she had become aware that many women were also in favour of a change. They were just too frightened of their menfolk to take a public stand.

In the days following the judgement, there was a marked difference in the attitude of some villagers towards her and a few did congratulate her discreetly, but only when the heat had abated somewhat. Heaping accolades on them, the media more than made up for the coolness with which the judgement was received by most people in Karoran. Seema and Chandrapati gave innumerable interviews and were projected as the heroines of the battle against social injustice in the state. The family became aware of the full significance of the judgement in the days that followed. Till then it was their private battle for seeking justice for Manoj and Babli, and they had little time to dwell on anything else. Though they still had no close friends in the village, Chandrapati and her three children had received a boost of badly needed confidence from the world outside.

Seema, in particular, also had the respectability of being a policewoman now, and often strode into Karoran in her uniform. It galled the traditionalists, who were sure that she wore the uniform to the village just to rub it in. Perhaps she did. She liked to walk up to the front door of her home and pause for a moment to see the effect on Chandrapati and Rekha. The two would look on in complete adoration. Seema ran the house and also paid part of the lawyer's expenses with her small salary of 14,000 rupees. She was their breadwinner, though Chandrapati continues to be the 'head of the house'. When Seema suggested something, Chandrapati immediately listened. So when she suggested that Chandrapati should defy the panchayat diktat to boycott the zila parishad elections, her mother took notice. She saw the boycott as a humiliation, designed to negate their victory.

'One boycott after another. Is this a joke? Are there no men in this village to drill sense into this senseless panchayat?' Chandrapati remarked, during their daily after-dinner banter.

Seema pulled down her cot from where it stood leaning against the wall. She spread a durrie on it and flung a pillow at one end, before flopping down. 'How can a handful of old fogeys decide on a boycott and force it on others? In those days they got away with such tactics against us. Things are not the same now. We should break their boycott,' she joined in.

Chandrapati stopped mending the torn sock she had in her hand, and looked up. 'A judicial court has given this judgement, not some kangaroo court like theirs and still they are in a twist.' For Rekha, this was the best time of the day, one she eagerly looked forward to. The household grind over, she came alive during these sessions.

'Ma, this is a challenge for you. Do it, do go and cast your vote tomorrow,' she egged her mother on, with an excited smile. Chandrapati loved a challenge and, with her newfound confidence, was itching to give it back too. But she had still not been able to handle the queasiness that seemed to rise from her stomach during difficult times in the last many months. She gave a vague nod and put away the torn socks she had meant to repair that evening. 'We'll see tomorrow. I am very tired today. Will sleep now.' And she pulled the sheet over her face. 'You girls, stop chattering. Vinod is studying in the other room.'

Seema had an off the next day and she and Rekha spent the morning persuading her to go to the polling station. They had heard from neighbours that the poll officials were whiling away their time playing cards because no one had come to vote. Towards noon, Chandrapati put on her cream plastic shoes and tossed an orange dupatta over her head. Rekha looked at Seema and smiled. The two sisters understood that something had finally snapped and their mother would go. They followed her till the door, where she asked the two police constables guarding them to come with her. Striding to the polling booth, flanked by them, Chandrapati looked impressive. Those who searched her face for anger and defiance were puzzled; it was expressionless. This was partly due to her nervousness because, for all her newfound bravado, Chandrapati knew that she wasn't entirely safe. She later told her daughters that their detractors were watching her every move with unconcealed animosity. They were there to enforce the diktat and prevent people from casting their votes, but made no attempt to stop her. She doesn't remember who she voted for, but does remember vaguely stamping on one symbol at the top of the ballot paper. It didn't matter. She wasn't there to elect anyone in particular, but to rub in a point. News of her defying the panchayat's diktat spread in Karoran within the next hour. But no one else came forward to vote and show solidarity with her. Towards evening, just as the bored polling staff began to call it a day, a merrily swaying Satpal, known in their patti as the village drunk, dittoed her action. Some laughed and said that he did it in a drunken fit and not to support Chandrapati. The panchayatis dismissed her action saying, 'What else could be expected from her? She has become a habitual opponent of anything that the panchayat does.'

At home that evening, Chandrapati had a smug smile on her face as she contemplated the flames in the hearth. With so much behind her, she could afford to indulge in a spot of anger. It wasn't a luxury for her any more. Oh, how she had enjoyed this indulgence.

*

June made way for a bounteous monsoon, and by the time winter set in, even the most arid of Haryana's districts were sated. The debate on honour crimes, triggered by the Manoj and Babli judgement, raged in the countryside and also in the national capital, Delhi. In Karoran, another kind of debate was taking place. Once again Chandrapati found herself in the midst of a controversy. In December 2010, the Haryana government decided to hold by-polls for those panchayats where elections had not been held. The slot for the sarpanch in Karoran was reserved for a woman candidate.

The norm in Haryana has been that the husband of the woman selected becomes a proxy for her, and for all practical purposes functions as the sarpanch. She rubber-stamps his decisions whenever she is free of her household duties. Since the khap panchayat actually calls the shots in the village, the ruse of having a unanimous candidate is often deployed, to place someone acceptable to the ruling clique. And, because the name is proposed by the khap panchayat, even dissenting villagers generally acquiesce. Since the previous sarpanch, Karambir, was from the influential Billa patti, this time the worthies from Meghan patti seized the initiative and proposed the name of Sucha Singh, a non-controversial farmer from their neighbourhood. Perhaps the absence of the powerful Gangaraj emboldened them.

Sucha Singh was in the Pundri grain market selling his paddy when he heard of his nomination. The news did not excite him. He was even irritated momentarily. Having a diploma in physical training, he was keen to get a job as an instructor. To be saddled with the duties of a sarpanch did not fit into his plans. The nomination was actually for his wife, Sudesh Rani, but her name was not even mentioned in the discussions. It was as if she didn't exist at all. The influential persons from his patti spent a few days to convince him, and once he took the decision to join, Sucha jumped in wholeheartedly. Hardly had his candidature been announced than the piqued Billa patti announced that Balla Ram of their locality would also contest. That meant that there would be an election and no unanimous selection.

By now Chandrapati was taking a keen interest in the panchayat matters, albeit from a distance. She did not like the idea of Balla Ram becoming the sarpanch. Babli was from Billa patti, and since the murders, no one from Chandrapati's family had ventured into that neighbourhood. 'We don't go to that patti at all. They are our enemies. If he becomes the sarpanch, it will be hard for us to get even a simple attestation done from him,' she articulated her fears before the family one day. 'That boy Darshan would have been a better candidate, but he is not contesting this time. Perhaps he is just fed up.'

The early-morning fog hadn't lifted from their little courtyard and Chandrapati's form was a shadow, as she washed her face and hands in a corner. She wiped her hands and took the tea Rekha had made for them. Sweet and milky, just as she liked it. Rekha sat cosily by the hearth, where she kneaded the dough for breakfast. 'Ma, this is a reserved seat for women. Why don't you stand for the election and become sarpanch? What fun it will be,' she said. Chandrapati stood dumbstruck, a chipped teacup in her hand. Rekha's words set her adrenalin surging and she flushed. She was standing with one hand on her hip and the other holding the cup. She pushed her right leg out and adjusted the weight of her body on to the other. She wagged the unburdened leg playfully in front of her and slowly loosened the plastic shoe on her foot. Seema recognized the gesture and realized that it was months, or was it years, since she had seen it. 'Ma is getting back her poise. Thank God for this judgement. It's made us normal again,' she thought.

'Rekha is right. If you stand for elections, yours will be the only genuine woman candidature. It will also prevent that Balla Ram from winning,' said she.

Chandrapati was thinking. 'Whether I win or not, at least I will know how many people actually support me in the village. Those who come to me under the cover of dusk to tell me that they are on my side will have to choose.'

*

In the following days, Chandrapati filled up her nomination form and was given the date palm as her election symbol. Rekha was beside herself with excitement. For once in her life she began to get impatient with her household duties and wanted to spend each waking moment in preparations for her mother's election. Seema drafted the contents of the pamphlet they had decided to print and distribute in the village. With a pen in her hand, she pondered over what all Chandrapati should promise. 'Let's say that you will work for the development of the village. Just like our grandfather did. Don't people remember him still? His memory will strike a chord with them.'

Vinod had his own idea of development. 'Do put in something about a playground for the village boys. The only ground is in school and, once I leave school, where will I play cricket?'

When the stack of pamphlets came from the press in Kaithal, still smelling of printer's ink, Rekha held it lovingly and made sure that not even one got lost. She went around the village lanes distributing them from house to house. Some houses did not open their doors to her, so she slipped it under their doors. At the same time, Chandrapati began visiting houses to seek support for herself, first in her own neighbourhood and then the others. She didn't bother going to Billa patti because as she told Seema one evening, 'It's no use wasting time there. They are hostile towards us and I'm sure Balla Ram will get all the votes from there.' She concentrated on the women and young men, whom she could count on for some support.

In a week's time it became clear that her candidature would divide the votes because she was becoming popular among the womenfolk. The advantage, everyone said, would go to Balla Ram and when Chandrapati heard of this she began to think. Sucha Singh was equally worried and he decided to discuss it with Chandrapati, to see if they could join hands. He was pleasantly surprised to discover that Chandrapati had made up her mind to stand down in his favour. 'Dekh, Sucha bhai, I only stood for the election to prevent Balla Ram from winning. If a split in votes benefits him, I would rather choose you than him. I have this much confidence that at least you won't support the khap against us now,' she said. That was that. Chandrapati was as good as her word.

On polling day, she stood with Sucha Singh and told her

supporters to vote for him. 'Bhai, Chandrapati is supporting me,' he kept telling the groups of women who came to cast their votes in the afternoon. His gesture of folded hands held above the head won the day and Sucha Singh is now the sarpanch of Karoran. Whenever Chandrapati visits his house, she gets a warm welcome and a cup of tea served by Sucha's mother herself. The last time she went, Sucha helped her to fill forms for getting an old-age pension.

*

In January 2011, exactly a year after her appointment, Jagmati resigned from the directorship of the women studies department of MDU, Rohtak. Her resignation was preceded by a whisper campaign in the university, as news about the complaints made to the vice chancellor had begun to circulate. It is odd how the best of people, despite good intentions, end up doing the opposite of what they mean to. When Jagmati resigned, Dr Hooda was a disappointed man. He tried to convince her to rethink her decision because, as he often shared with other professors, 'No one is more suited than her to head this department. She is the right person for it and our university is fortunate to have her here.'

But Jagmati was not going back. She was clear that she would have to chart another course. 'I shouldn't have taken it up in the first place. Such positions are not for women like me,' she told Inderjeet that evening at home. 'They say I am unconventional and rigid. If raising a voice against such injustice is being unconventional, then so be it. At one level, I am glad to be rid of the responsibility, because it was taking up a lot of my time.'

Inderjeet didn't comment. He sensed that she didn't even want him to. He became a listening post.

'Now we can follow up on the Karnal judgement and use

the momentum to push for a law against honour killings. The events of the last few months have bogged us down and our energies are being spent more on defending ourselves.'

*

The Madhuban police training academy near Karnal is an eighty-hectare leafy sprawl on the national highway. Besides training recruits for the Haryana police, the academy also conducts courses for probationer officers of the Indian Police Service (IPS) doing the state leg of their training. Ever since Seema was recruited she had spent most of her time here, first during training, and now on duty. She had a small two-room flat on the campus which she still hadn't bothered to do up. Home for her was the village and, at every opportunity, she rushed back to be with the family.

One cold winter day, someone came to the academy, looking for a 'Karoran ki Babli'. Two constables, Surendra and Sandeep, were heading for duty at the canteen in the academy complex when they bumped into a scruffy, trembling man, who stopped them to ask where he could find this person. Sandeep at once guessed that the man was looking for Seema and told him, 'There is a Karoran ki Seema here, not Babli.'

'Yes, yes, that's right. Seema. Who are you?' the man stammered.

'I am Seema's colleague. You must be looking for her.' The man, who identified himself as Virender, seemed upset on hearing this.

'Oh, okay. But you don't tell her that I am searching for her. I'll ask someone else the way to her room,' he said and began to walk towards a block of residential flats.

Sandeep and Surendra exchanged looks. They both knew Seema well and were aware of the circumstances in which she had taken up this job. They thought the man somewhat odd and felt they should find out more about him.

'*Baat sun, bhai*. The girl you are searching for will be coming to the canteen in a short while. Why don't you come and have tea there, till she comes?' said Sandeep. He strode up to Virender, took him by the elbow and steered him away from the flats. To his surprise, the man did not resist.

In this cold, people demanded hot tea and coffee. So they were surprised when Virender asked for a cold drink. His hands shook as he held the bottle of Coke they gave him. Sandeep joined him with his own steaming cup of tea and decided to try out his recently acquired skills as an investigating cop. He didn't have to try very hard. For some reason, Virender seemed eager to unburden himself.

'I have come to kill Seema,' he told them within two minutes of sitting down. They looked on disbelievingly, and waited for him to say more. He lifted his shirt and showed them the katta (country-made pistol) he had procured from Uttar Pradesh. 'But don't tell anyone,' he said haltingly. This is recorded in the FIR Seema filed later. Further, it stated that he had instructions from one Rishi to deal with two targets, one here and the other in Delhi.

The stunned cops realized that they had trouble on their hands and that they would have to warn Seema. The man was sweating despite the cold and seemed unstable. He was having difficulty speaking. He seemed to be under the influence of a potent narcotic. In his present condition they doubted if he would be able to fire two straight bullets at Seema's flat, let alone at her. They guessed that the drug had probably fuddled his instincts and made him blabber out his plan. But still, she had to be warned. A few minutes later, around 3 p.m., Sandeep spotted Seema leaving her flat, and she was walking past the canteen, on the way to her duty shift. Surendra stopped her and she came in reluctantly to hear what he had to say.

'I'm getting late for duty. What is it, Surendra?' she said irritably.

'Someone wants to see you, Seema. He is sitting in the canteen.'

Seema had her back to Virender and whispered to Surendra that she didn't have the time for it just now. And before 'the man' could turn around to look at her, she walked out of the canteen.

At work, she wondered who it was. 'Possibly it was someone with yet another compromise formula.' She decided that she would go back to the canteen after her shift and ask Sandeep and Surendra.

Back at the canteen, Virender was restless. 'It's getting late. I will come day after tomorrow now. But you mustn't tell her that I came,' he told the cops and left.

An evening mist had begun to swirl by the time Seema returned from work. It was cold and she hurried towards her flat, thinking she would call up Sandeep and ask him about the visitor, once she reached home. On second thoughts, she stopped near the canteen and went in to look for him. Both Sandeep and Surendra were waiting for her and quickly filled her in on what they had learned. 'Be careful, Seema. This is looking quite dangerous.' He handed her Virender's identity card, which they had managed to extract from him. They told her that Virender was serving a sentence in Ambala jail, where the convicted men from Karoran were also held. 'He was high on drugs, Seema. That is why he babbled out the purpose of his visit. He is on parole from jail and the convicts from your village have given him the task of killing you. We think you should not waste any time in lodging a complaint at the police station. Inform IG sahib at the earliest, before this Virender returns, fortified,' said Sandeep worried.

'This is it. They have come for me.' She shivered at the realization. For many months now, through the days when she was running from pillar to pillar, Seema had heard rumours to this effect. 'They have killed Manoj, but you are the root, which is still living and fighting back. They might be in jail, but they will not let you and Chandrapati live in peace,' she had been told by many people in the village. It was a fear she had pushed to the furthest corner of her mind. The constant march of events, dealing with the court case and their own precarious financial condition hardly gave her much time to reflect on such a possibility. But here it was, clear and present. Could Virender's appearance here and his bumbling incoherence just be a warning from them, or was he actually going to execute his plan? She couldn't tell. She could feel her head becoming heavy and her mind clouded over as she tried desperately to grapple with the problem at hand.

That night when Seema spoke to her mother on the phone, a chill crept around Chandrapati's heart. 'Dear God, how much more will we be tested?' she thought. Her mind went back to their after-dinner conversation two nights ago. It was odd. Though they all must have felt it subconsciously, it was Rekha, with her knack for drawing attention to the obvious, who had observed that each time things began to take a turn for the better something happened to send them scurrying for cover again. No one had responded immediately; they seemed to be ruminating over what she had said. Eventually, Chandrapati dealt her a gentle reprimand. *'Rekha, bas bhi kar. Ab kya hoga?'* She was superstitious about such talk, as if trouble, hanging in the air, might invite itself on hearing its name.

'Talk of the devil and here it is,' she thought, as she put down the phone. 'This girl Rekha, couldn't she keep her mouth shut?' Chandrapati had no doubts about who wanted

Seema eliminated. She thanked Providence the operation was botched. But her heart kept saying, 'Next time Seema may not be so lucky.'

The next day Seema registered an FIR at the Madhuban police station and a few days later Virender was arrested in Delhi. The matter was widely reported in the newspapers and some news channels also managed to speak with Virender in custody. He admitted on camera that he had struck up an acquaintance with Rajinder and others in jail who had promised to give him 25 lakh rupees if he killed Seema. Someone asked him why he had not done so. Still incoherent and trembling, Virender replied, 'She is lucky. I just did not get an opportunity, or else I would have done it.'

Soon after the Karnal court judgement, the district police had stepped up the security of Seema and her family in Karoran. They have two cops guarding them round the clock. A police post has been established in the village and cops also patrol the village lanes. After Virender's attempt to kill her was exposed, the Kaithal police reviewed their security cover and added a police control room (PCR) van, which transports them whenever they have to go outside the village. The same PCR van fetches Seema from Madhuban on weekends.

The police keeps a watchful eye on them at all times. Seema chaffs when occasionally the security cocoon becomes claustrophobic. Like the time she argued with her seniors in Madhuban when they were jittery about letting her go home every weekend. For the government, and the police machinery in particular, the safety of Chandrapati's family is a reluctant mission, something they would rather not be involved in. The law that they uphold may stumble in execution. Hasn't Chandrapati seen it all at play? The family has learned not to become too friendly with their guards. Their house has got divided into the space occupied by the guards, which is the front end, near the buffaloes, and the rear courtyard and rooms, which are theirs as before. Sometimes the policemen climb the stairs to reach the terrace when they want a smoke or to gossip. The most uncomfortable part of this arrangement is the access to the tiny toilet which is situated in the guards' portion of the house. The three women of the house have learned to cover their head and lower their eyes when they go to use the toilet. 'It's a small price to pay to stay alive,' they tell themselves. The security hasn't given them back their earlier carefree life, but still it is something that helps them sleep better at night. The irony of their cosseted situation, though, distresses Chandrapati every day. 'The government is spending so much money to protect us from our oppressors now. If only they had guarded my Manoj and Babli with the same zeal,' she muses.

Epilogue

Two months after the Karnal court's judgement, Chandrapati filed an appeal in the Punjab and Haryana High Court. She pleaded that Gangaraj should be given the death penalty like the others on the ground that he 'not only master-minded the entire murder plan but was also present on the spot at the time of murder of Manoj and Babli'. Her appeal also sought a life sentence for Mandeep and an enhancement of the compensation of 1 lakh rupees that Gangaraj had been directed to pay her.

On 11 March 2011, the high court acquitted Gangaraj and Satish of the charges against them and commuted the death sentences of the remaining into life imprisonment. The court held that the presence of Gangaraj on the scene of the crime was not established; hence the charges against him do not stand. Satish Kumar was let off because the court felt that the prosecution could not establish that he was the son of Babli's maternal uncle. Both Gangaraj and Satish were released.

The high court declined to confirm the death sentences of Baru Ram, Suresh, Rajinder and Gurdev, taking a view that since the entire case of the prosecution depended on circumstantial evidence, the court has had to infer certain facts from the projected circumstances. Lastly, it came down heavily on the investigating agency (police) for bungling at every step of this sensational case. 'We are constrained to infer that the police officials had been hand in glove with the accused party and provided loopholes at every stage of investigation . . . we find that they had just investigated the matter for the purpose of giving disposal to the investigation.' It directed the director general of police to initiate disciplinary proceedings against SI Jagbir Singh, then SHO of Rajaund police station, HC Dharampal and HC Subhash for investigating the case in a casual manner.

The khaps rejoiced at the judgement. 'An injustice has been set right,' they said. But Chandrapati preferred an appeal before the Supreme Court to get Gangaraj and Satish convicted again. Her appeal is also against the commutation of death penalty to life imprisonment for the others. The appeal was admitted by the Supreme Court in November 2011.

Gangaraj returned to Karoran a bitter person. The perceived let-down by the Congress party, which forced him to surrender before the police, still rankles. He shuns politics and doesn't meet journalists any more. But his release has made Chandrapati and her family insecure again. So has the knowledge that the others who are serving their sentences are often out on parole.

Vinod still does not attend regular college in Kaithal and is appearing for his BA papers privately. Rekha is doing the same with Plus Two exams. As for Seema, she doesn't want to be a police constable any more. She has set her eyes on the state judicial services and took leave from work to attend coaching classes in Delhi. Whenever she reflects on their journey from being the hounded to the protected, there is some satisfaction. But life for them is still bitter, still threatened. 'This is our destiny. Everyone sees their punishment, their jail terms. No one notices our punishment, our confinement, our fears . . .'

The exposure of the plot to eliminate Seema has convinced them that their troubles are not yet over. Will Chandrapati leave her home in Karoran and seek a safe haven elsewhere? She doesn't have an answer as yet.

Afterword

The barbaric and medieval tradition of honour killing has been around for long, but the public discourse on it is barely a decade old. Are we seeing a revival of this hoary practice? Or is it just that murder for honour has caught the fancy of the media and what was anyway happening in the countryside and even urban centres is now being made public due to competitive reportage? I would think it is a little of both.

The 'honour' of a clan or caste, particularly in landed communities, has always been linked with its women. Consequently, these societies have traditionally dealt with indiscretions and assertions of sexuality by their women with a heavy hand. It would be reasonable to assume that the rebellious were few and far between until a couple of decades ago, mainly because young couples asserting themselves to choose their own partners hadn't become the trend it now is even in rural areas. The influence of 24 x 7 soaps and interaction between boys and girls in schools, colleges and in the workplace have strengthened this. Liberalization of the economy has led to the movement of the young beyond the boundaries of their districts to towns and metros for work, exposing them to newer social realities and norms. Not only is this the reason why the young are beginning to question their old social mores, the resultant physical distance between them and their ancestral roots has encouraged them to believe that they can take liberties with the taboos and traditions they grew up with. Unfortunately, the attempts of the young to unshackle themselves from some of these traditions has coincided with the waning influence of khaps, who have taken it upon themselves to combat the increasingly viral love bug, if only to ensure their own survival.

With modern democratic institutions taking over almost all their earlier roles, khap panchayats are left with little else except deep-rooted, traditional notions of honour to retain legitimacy in a world where there is no room for extra-constitutional bodies like theirs. The bizarre fatwas that make it routinely to the newspaper headlines have to be seen then as the desperate bid of khap panchayats to hold on to the clout that was once theirs.

So, though killing for honour, with social sanction, is invoked as an ancient, time-tested tradition to justify it today, this should be seen more as a symptom of the clash between the old and the evolving new social norms that appear to be overturning ancient kinship rules. The transformation is taking place at a rate faster than social institutions like the khaps or even political parties can keep up with, and governments in these states, sensitive to caste concerns, are reluctant to assert the rule of law. The standard tactic to deal with demands from enlightened members of civil society, activists or rival parties is to go into denial mode or profess ignorance about the existence of such crimes.

This was borne out in the Manoj and Babli case. It is also true in more instances of honour crimes that have come to light in recent years. These are only a few of them.

We have earlier touched upon the case of Vedpal Maun, a twenty-seven-year-old medical practitioner of Mataur village in Kaithal district, who was lynched to death on

22 July 2009 by a huge crowd led by wife Sonia's family members, even though he was accompanied by a warrant officer, Suraj Bhan, appointed by the Punjab and Haryana High Court, and a posse of policemen. The law enforcers were also attacked by the villagers. Vedpal had gone to recover Sonia from her village, when his in-laws refused to send her back after marriage, and she sent him a desperate message that her parents were harassing her.

Vedpal and Sonia, both from the Jat community, were from different gotras and lived in adjacent villages. When they fell in love and realized that there would be opposition to their marriage, they eloped and got married in Chandigarh under the Hindu Marriage Act. The Banwala gotra (to which Sonia belonged) khap held a series of meetings and declared a 'reward' for the murder of the couple. The khap's argument was that even though they belonged to different gotras, the norms of bhaichara between the two villages of Singhwal and Mataur ruled out any conjugal relations between them.

Following Vedpal's death, Sonia was forced to state that she had been coerced into the marriage. An FIR was registered by Vedpal's family and on 29 September 2011 the district and sessions court of Jind convicted twelve of the fourteen accused, which include Sonia's father, Dhanraj, and some khap members. They have been given life imprisonment. Pavanjit Banwala, the head of the All India Adarsh Jat Mahasabha, was acquitted as there was insufficient evidence against him. Sonia's mother, Dhanpati, who for about two years was reportedly absconding, has been arrested recently and the case against her is still in the court.

In yet another case, Sonia and Rampal, who are from the same village of Asandh in Rohtak district, were declared by the Rathi khap as brother and sister in 2004 and ordered to dissolve their marriage. They had been married for one and a half years and Sonia was three months pregnant. Their crime was that they had defied the principle of village exogamy which prohibits marriages between people from the same village. Rampal is from the Dahiya gotra, while Sonia is a Rathi. Three khap members including the elected sarpanch of a nearby village went to Rampal's house and manhandled Sonia. The sarpanch pulled off her veil saying that since she is a daughter of the village, she need not wear it like other married women do. They told her to accept the token eleven rupees from Rampal, meant to sanctify their relationship as a brother and sister, but she refused.

The physical and mental intimidation led to premature labour and Sonia had to be hospitalized. The khap even offered to take the responsibility for getting her married again. No action was taken against the khap members until the People's Union for Civil Liberties filed a public interest petition in the high court. The two-judge bench of Chief Justice B.K. Roy and Justice Suryakant directed the deputy commissioner and superintendent of police to provide security to the couple and directed that neither the panchayat nor anyone else should interfere in the married life of the couple.

Violation of the bhaichara taboo between gotras laid down by khaps came up when Ravinder Gehlaut of Dharana village in Jhajjar district married Shilpa, a Kadyan girl from Panipat district in 2009. Ravinder had lived for most of his life in Sultanpur in Delhi with his aunt who had adopted him at a very young age. In July 2009 Ravinder went to Dharana to attend a marriage. Dharana and some other surrounding villages are dominated by the Kadyan gotra and, by this reckoning, the Kadyan khap of that area decreed that since Shilpa is a Kadyan she could only be a sister to Ravinder. Curiously, activists of the Janwadi Mahila Samiti detected that in the same village there are about ten families where a boy from the Kadyan gotra has married a girl belonging to the Gehlauts. But the khap was unbending. It directed that the couple should annul their marriage or 'face the consequences'.

On 13 July 2009 the Kadyan khap began an indefinite protest demanding the ouster of the family from the village as Ravinder and Shilpa had not annulled their marriage. On 19 July the Gehlauts left the village and villagers tried to stone their house. There was a clash between them and the police. The Gehlaut family approached the Punjab and Haryana High Court for protection against their oppressors and sought action against the khap members for issuing diktats to end the marriage. Ravinder was so traumatized with the harassment that he attempted suicide by consuming poison. He survived due to some timely medical help. The Gehlauts later returned to the village with a heavy police protection but the family lives in fear.

Ravinder is very bitter about the role played by the police and the polity in his case. 'Initially, the police and administration rendered no help at all and remained silent spectators, as if nothing had happened. In fact the SHO of Beri police station even suggested to me that I should divorce Shilpa and remarry, instead of bearing so much trouble. The Hooda-led government in Haryana flatly refused to come to our support. Deepender Hooda [the chief minister's son and Lok Sabha MP from Rohtak] clearly stated that since this is a social issue, he could not intervene in it.'

*

Where does all this leave the bill for a separate law to deal with 'honour killings' that the Central government was pushed into by the conviction, the first ever, of the accused in the Manoj–Babli case?

A month after the Karnal judgement, Law Minister Veerappa Moily declared in April 2010 that the government has prepared a draft bill which seeks to amend several related acts such as the Indian Evidence Act, 1872, the Indian Penal Code and the Criminal Procedure Code to bring honour killings under the ambit of the law. Among other things, it aimed at amending Section 105 of the Indian Evidence Act by shifting the burden of proof on the accused in a reversal of the principles of criminal justice. India's anti-dowry laws already allow for such an exception. In the case of honour killings, the onus would be on khaps, family members and other perpetrators of honour crimes like abettors in the village to establish that they were not guilty. The bill also sought the introduction of a fifth clause to Section 300 of the Indian Penal Code which defines murder. The new definition would make 'honour killings' dictated by khap panchayats a distinct offence, and all community members who participate in its illegal proceedings, not just those who carry out the orders to murder, would be held guilty.

It was also proposed to amend the Special Marriage Act, 1954, to reduce the notice period which couples have to give before registration of their marriage from the present one month to nil. This was felt necessary because in most cases where couples run away from home to get married, the crucial one-month notice period enables their relatives to track them down and force them into submission. It was seen that this situation usually results in the death of the girl, which the family members mostly resort to, to restore their honour and standing in society, sullied by her elopement.

Sadly, the proposed law, which was hailed across the country by those working against honour crimes, has got mired in objections from many central ministers and states such as Haryana. Here's how it happened.

In July 2010, taking into account the serious divisions in the Cabinet on the proposed law, the Central government set up a Group of Ministers (GoM) to suggest changes in the law and also decided to consult the states before proceeding ahead. Some ministers had reservations on the proposed bill as they felt that khap panchayats' pressure against marriages within the gotra, village or outside the community have social sanction. There were also doubts as to whether, when a whole congregation of villagers was involved in ordering a killing, all of them could be held accountable and how. Besides, to implement any change in the laws, the Centre is dependent on the states. It was considered necessary to consult them.

Haryana was the first to strongly oppose the proposed amendment bill. In a letter dated 25 August 2010, Chief Minister Bhupinder Singh Hooda wrote to Pranab Mukherjee heading the GoM, in which he gave a point by point rebuttal to all the proposed amendments. The crux of his argument was that the existing laws are adequate to deal with the problem. The chief minister felt that rephrasing legal provisions may not really help and shifting the burden of proof on the suspected offenders would hurt the cause of justice.

The matter was referred to the Law Commission of India and in January 2012 the commission rejected all proposals to amend Section 300 of the IPC. It said that not only were the available provisions adequate to prosecute all types of murders but also warned against overturning universally accepted principles of jurisprudence. The commission instead drafted another bill which seeks to prohibit unlawful assemblies that interfere with legally valid marriages and charges all those present at such assemblies with non-bailable offences, a two-year jail term and a fine.

Those fighting for a separate law to deal with honour

crimes see the Law Commission's draft bill as a vastly diluted legislation, which may not be strong enough to address the problem. It is quite obvious that the political impact of a specific legislation in the khap-dominated parts of North India is the overriding concern.

But even as the government prevaricates, the Supreme Court on 19 April 2011 took a strong step and described khaps as 'illegal and unconstitutional'. A bench of the apex court comprising of Justice Markandey Katju and Gyan Sudha Mishra held that honour killings fell in the category of rarest of rare cases, deserving of a death sentence. In doing so, it cleared many ambiguities which lower courts encounter while dealing with such crimes, and laid out a clear, definite path for them and the administrative machinery to follow. It said that district magistrates and superintendents of police in the districts would be held directly liable for their failure to stop khap panchayats from acting like kangaroo courts which order or encourage the killing of couples exercising their choice of marriage partners. Criminal proceedings should also be taken against officials if they failed to apprehend the culprits and institute criminal charges against khap members after they harmed or killed hapless couples, the court said. Justice Markandey Katju's ruling came while adjudicating a case from Tamil Nadu in which the court went into the illegalities committed by caste panchayats, known in North India as khap panchayats and in Tamil Nadu as katta panchayats.

A copy of the judgement was sent to all state chief secretaries, district magistrates and superintendents of police. On 9 May 2011 the same bench of the Supreme Court followed up by once again describing honour killings as the 'rarest of rare' cases, deserving of a death sentence. 'This is necessary as a deterrent for such outrageous, uncivilised behaviour. All persons who are planning to perpetrate "honour" killings should know that the gallows await them,' said the bench. The observation assumed significance because the usual punishment for murder convicts is life imprisonment and the death sentence is awarded only in the rarest of rare cases. The judgement has created 'honour killings' as a separate genre warranting a death sentence, and leaves very little room for judges to exercise their discretion in deciding the quantum of punishment in such cases. It is two years since the draft of the proposed amendment bill meant to provide a legal framework to address honour crimes in the country was prepared. The court has stepped into an area where the government failed to deliver so far.

Khap panchayats of Haryana have already rubbished the Supreme Court rulings by taking the stand that they do not apply to them! But activists and eloping couples have drawn much strength from the rulings, and it is becoming increasingly apparent that those who kill for honour may not find the going as easy as before. The spotlight that all these developments have brought on the plight of young couples who choose their own partners has also pushed the Haryana government to set up 'protection homes' for them in the districts. These 'homes' have become hugely popular, as they provide a safe shelter during the critical one month or so after a couple elopes and gets married. This does not mean that honour killings are going to end any time soon. Men and women are still killed for defying kinship taboos in Haryana and Punjab. Some cases get reported but most still do not. The ones that reach the courts are a minuscule percentage. Until the government frames a strong law to deal with honour crimes, the malaise will continue to afflict these societies.